THE DEVELOPMEMT OF WESTERN CIVILIZATION

Narrative Essays in the History of Our Tradition
from the Greek City-States to the Present

EDITED BY EDWARD W. FOX

The Rise of the
Feudal Monarchies

BY SIDNEY PAINTER

The Rise of the Feudal Monarchies

SIDNEY PAINTER

THE JOHNS HOPKINS UNIVERSITY

*

Cornell University Press

ITHACA, NEW YORK

Introduction

THE proposition that each generation must rewrite history is more widely quoted than practiced. In the field of college texts on western civilization, the conventional accounts have been revised and sources and supplementary materials have been developed; but it is too long a time since the basic narrative has been rewritten to meet the rapidly changing needs of new college generations. In the mid-twentieth century such an account must be brief, well written, based on unquestioned scholarship, and assume almost no previous historical knowledge on the part of the reader. It must provide a coherent analysis of the development of western civilization and its basic values. It must, in short, constitute a systematic introduction to the collective memory of that tradition we are being asked to defend. This series of narrative essays has been undertaken in an effort to provide such a text for the introductory history survey course offered in the College of Arts and Sciences of Cornell University. It is being published in this form in the belief that the requirements of this one course reflect a need that is coming to be widely recognized.

Now that it is no longer practical to expect college freshmen to possess knowledge of classic languages or civilizations, any real familiarity with the Bible, any acquaintance with the great historical novels, or to have had any formal instruction in non-American history, it is imperative that texts in the history of European civilization be fully self-explanatory. To meet this need it was decided to focus the essays on a bold outline of those major trends and developments that have led from the beginning of our recorded time to the most pressing of our present problems. This meant that names and events which did not take an integral place in the account—no matter how firmly they might be embedded in historical protocol—had to be deleted. It did not mean that the intellectual level of presentation need be lowered; in fact, every effort has been made to raise it. Each contributor has been urged to write for a mature audience, and it is hoped, therefore, that the essays may prove profitable and rewarding to readers outside the college classroom.

It is the plan of the first part of the series to sketch the narrative of our history from its origins in the city-states of ancient Greece to the eve of the French Revolution in related essays, each written by a recognized scholar, to serve as the basic reading for one week in a semester course. The developments of the nineteenth and twentieth centuries will be covered in a succeeding series which will provide the same quantity of reading material for each week of the second semester. This scale of presentation has been adopted in the conviction that any understanding of the central problem of the preservation of the integrity and dignity of the individual human being depends first on an examination of its origins in the politics and philosophy of the ancient Greeks and the religion of the ancient Hebrews, and then on an increasingly detailed knowledge of the more recent developments leading to the industrial urban society of today.

The decision to devote equal space to twenty-five centuries and to a century and a half was based on the analogy with the human memory. Those events most remote tend to be remembered in least detail but often with a sense of clarity and perspective that is absent in more recent and more crowded recollections. If the roots of our tradition must be identified, their relation to the present must be carefully developed. The nearer the narrative approaches contemporary times, the more difficult and complicated this becomes. Recent experience must be worked over more carefully and in more detail if it is to contribute effectively to an understanding of the contemporary world.

It may be objected that the series attempts too much. The attempt is being made, however, on the assumption that any historical development should be susceptible of meaningful treatment on any scale and in the realization that a very large proportion of today's college students do not have more time to invest in this part of their education. The practical alternative appears to lie between some attempt to create a new brief account of the history of our tradition and the abandonment of any serious effort to communicate the essence of that tradition to all but a handful of our students. It is the conviction of everyone contributing to this series that the second alternative must not be accepted by default.

In a series covering such a vast sweep of time, few scholars would find themselves thoroughly at home in the fields covered by more than one or two of the essays. This meant, in practice, that almost every essay should be written by a different author. In spite of apparent drawbacks, this procedure promised real advantages. Each contributor would be in a position to set higher standards of accuracy and insight in an essay encompassing a major portion of the field of his life's work than could ordinarily be expected in surveys of some ten or twenty centuries. The inevitable discontinuity of style and interpretation could be modified by editorial co-ordination; but it was felt that some discontinuity was in itself desirable. No illusion is more easily acquired by the student in an elementary course, or is more prejudicial to the efficacy of such a course, than that a single smoothly articulated text represents the very substance of history itself. If the shift from author to author, week by week, raises difficulties for the beginning student, they are difficulties that will not so much impede his progress as contribute to his growth.

This essay, *The Rise of the Feudal Monarchies* by Mr. Sidney Painter, is the third of the series to be published. It provides a rapid but careful survey of the principal events connected with the accretion of territorial bases and development of institutional foundations for three of the great political sovereignties of modern Europe. This is an early, but none the less important, chapter in the story of the growth of political units which has dominated much of European history and now in the mid-twentieth century approaches a final climax.

EDWARD WHITING FOX

Princeton, New Jersey
January, 1951

Contents

Prolegomena

DURING the seventh, eighth, ninth, and tenth centuries the dominant form of government in western Europe was what has come to be known as "Germanic" monarchy. There were two quite different types—the primitive and the more fully developed. From very early times the various Germanic peoples had been accustomed to choose chieftains to lead them in war. When the state of war was prolonged, these chieftains tended to become permanent and to bolster their position with mythical traditions of a divine origin. Thus the Merovingian kings and the Anglo-Saxon rulers of Wessex claimed descent from Germanic gods. These early Germanic monarchies were in theory elective, but custom usually confined eligibility for election to the members of a single family. The royal power rested on three bases. Each king had a small group of men, bound to him by special oaths of loyalty, who served as his officials and bodyguard, clearly a later form of the German chieftain's *comitatus*. Then, as the leader of his people in time of war, he had the right to call every able-bodied man to military service. Finally, since there was no taxation, the king's material resources came chiefly from the land he had reserved for his own use. In time of peace his governmental functions were extremely limited. The administration of justice was carried on by the people themselves in their popular courts, and the king's local officials were mere supervisors. Outside of fighting, the chief occupations of the early Germanic kings were keeping up their supply of wine and concubines.

This simple conception of kingship began to change as soon as it came into contact with the Christian church. The political ideas of the church had their origins in Hellenistic civilization. The Hellenistic king, the *basileus*, had been a sacred person—he was not a god, but he was more nearly divine than ordinary men. In Christian thought the king became a man appointed by God to rule over his fellows. Although the Christian conception of kingship is seen most clearly in the Byzantine monarchy, it had a profound effect on the Germanic kingdoms of the West. Churchmen did not think of the king as a mere war chief with a few special privileges in time of peace. To them he had been appointed by God to keep order, protect the weak from the strong, and especially to maintain the Christian church and faith. Consistently and firmly throughout these centuries of confusion that have been called the Dark Ages, the church not only supported the kings against any forces that threatened their position but regularly preached the sanctity of kingly office. The later Germanic monarchs drew a large part of their resources from the lands of the church and relied heavily on ecclesiastics in the royal administration. This transformation of Germanic kings to Christian priest-kings was, of course, slow and gradual. The process began with the conversion of the Germanic peoples and was early symbolized in the crowning and anointing of Pepin as king of the Franks by the pope, even though the culmination of this alliance between church and monarchy was not reached until the early eleventh century under the Salian emperors.

In the last years of the tenth century Germanic monarchies of one or the other of these two types ruled most of Europe. The more primitive form was represented by the governments of Denmark, Norway, Sweden, and Kievan Russia. Anglo-Saxon England and the Holy Roman Empire that embraced Germany, Italy, and the eastern part of modern France were monarchies of the more advanced type. Although western France under the last of the Carolingians had highly developed feudal institutions, it was still in theory a Germanic monarchy.

In the course of the tenth, eleventh, and twelfth centuries the three great Germanic monarchies, England, France, and Germany, were profoundly changed by the development of the feudal institutions that have been described in an earlier essay in this series. At different times and under different circumstances they were transformed into what historians call feudal monarchies. The term feudal monarchy has been used so loosely by many writers that it is extremely difficult to define in terms of current usage. In general, one can say that a feudal state is one in which all the members of the ruling class form a feudal hierarchy with a chief lord or suzerain at its peak. If one wants to include the crusaders' states (the Latin kingdom of Jerusalem, the kingdom of Cyprus, and the Latin empire of Constantinople) among the feudal monarchies, it is necessary to say that all that is required to make a feudal state into a feudal monarchy is to have the suzerain bear the title of king. The rulers of these kingdoms had no power or resources that were not derived from their position in the feudal hierarchy. But in the three great states of western Europe the rulers retained in theory at least the authority of the Germanic kings and their power as feudal suzerains was complementary. This was also true of the Norman kingdom of Sicily even though it had not been preceded by a Germanic kingdom. Then in some states there were feudal elements but no completely organized feudal hierarchy. This situation was a stage in the development of feudal monarchy in England, France, and Germany. The Scandinavian kingdoms, Kievan Russia, and the Spanish kingdoms reached this stage but never became full feudal monarchies.

The object of this essay is to trace the development of the three great western states during the later Middle Ages, to follow their transformation from Germanic to feudal monarchies, and to indicate the forces that were to make England a constitutional, France an absolute, and Germany a figurehead monarchy. Although the chief focus of the essay must be on the depiction of an important phase of the political history of western civilization, it should be borne in mind constantly that the subject is by no means purely academic. Many of the problems that face Europe today have their roots in the Middle Ages. And the origins of Anglo-American political ideas and institutions are deeply embedded in the history of the English feudal monarchy.

CHAPTER I

France

THE Frankish kingdom ruled by Charlemagne was a Germanic monarchy of the advanced type. The backbone of his army consisted of *vassi dominici*, men who had been given land in return for military service and who had sworn a special oath of loyalty to the king. But the mass of his host was composed of the ordinary freemen of the realm. The king's material resources came chiefly from the royal estates scattered through the country. The central administration consisted of a relatively small group of magnates both lay and ecclesiastical. These men were entrusted with special missions of all sorts and were sent out as *missi dominici* to supervise the conduct of the realm. The king's local agents were the counts. In the western part of the empire they actually ruled as the king's representatives over districts that in general coincided with the former Roman *civitates*. In the east they did little more than supervise the local popular courts. Although the great mass of law enforced in the state was ancient custom—Roman or Germanic according to the region—the king could issue decrees that had the force of law. Charlemagne worked in close alliance with the church and relied heavily on its aid in keeping order, especially in such newly conquered regions as Saxony. As he appointed the bishops and abbots, the clergy was in many respects a branch of the royal administration. The Carolingian kingdom was far removed from the primitive Germanic monarchy of the Merovingians, yet, unfortunately, it had retained two of its chief characteristics. The succession to the crown was still in theory by election and it was considered proper to divide the realm among all a king's sons.

The century and a half that followed Charlemagne's death in 814 was a period of almost incredible confusion in the western part of his realm. The members of the Carolingian house quarreled fiercely over the crown, the royal estates, and the services of the *vassi dominici*. Wild Viking raiders plundered the coasts, sailed up the rivers, and ravaged the entire countryside. Moslems from Spain established themselves in the delta of the Rhône and plundered the region. The various parts of the state could defend themselves only through the development of a feudal hierarchy. The *vassi dominici* and ordinary landholders who had depended directly on the king became the vassals of the counts. Weak counts became the vassals of stronger ones. At the same time the offices of the counts and the fiefs of the *vassi dominici* became hereditary. The great ecclesiastical estates on which the Carolingian dynasty depended heavily for support were also seriously weakened. Great lords like the counts of Toulouse, the dukes of Aquitaine, and the dukes of Normandy simply usurped the crown's ancient rights over the church and appointed bishops and abbots themselves. Lesser lords forced the ecclesiastics to give them large parts of their lands as fiefs. Still others accepted the obligation of protecting a bishopric or abbey in return for control of its resources. The last kings of the Carolingian dynasty were almost helpless. The royal estates had been reduced to the town of Laon. The monarchs controlled only a few sadly depleted episcopal sees and abbeys. The great feudal lords acknowledged that the king was their suzerain, but he was completely unable to enforce the rights that went with that position. And although he could and did issue decrees, no one paid any attention to them.

Hugh Capet

The weakness of the Carolingian kings made it almost inevitable that some of the great lords of France should be tempted to try to gain the throne. As the monarchy was elective in theory, they were inclined to make it so in practice. In 888 a group of magnates, moved chiefly by the fact that all the available Carolingians were minors and that the defense of the realm against the Vikings required an able soldier, elected as king Odo, count of Paris, who ruled for ten years. In 922 Odo's brother, Robert, was elected king and

ruled for a year. Then the magnates chose Ralph, duke
of Burgundy, who was king for thirteen years. Thus
between Charlemagne's death in 814 and 987 three
men who were not members of the Carolingian house
were elected king of the West Franks. In 987 the same
process was repeated—the great lords chose Hugh
Capet, grandson of Robert and grandnephew of Odo.
It seems clear that as far as the great lords were concerned the monarchy had become fully elective. When
a king died, they would meet to choose his successor.
Under these conditions there was little fear that the
king would be more than the head of the feudal hierarchy.

Fortunately for the future of the French monarchy,
Hugh Capet was determined to make the royal office
hereditary in his own family. Shortly after his coronation he announced that the task of governing and defending the realm was too great for one man and
demanded that the magnates elect his son Robert as his
associate on the throne. This device effectively assured
Robert of being his father's successor. The practice of
having the king's eldest son elected and crowned during his lifetime became a custom of the Capetian house
and was only abandoned when the monarchy became
strong enough to render it no longer necessary. But
this method of negating the elective principal could
only be effective as long as the reigning house could
supply a male heir. The descendants of Hugh Capet
have been astoundingly successful in this respect. One

of Hugh's titles before he became king, that of count of Paris, is today borne by his direct descendant in the male line—the current pretender to the throne of France.

The Royal Demesne

As we have seen, the great vassals of the crown had deprived the Carolingian kings of all sources of power. In 987 six feudal potentates held all France except the tiny royal demesne around Laon: the count of Flanders, the duke of Normandy, the duke of France, the duke of Burgundy, the duke of Aquitaine, and the count of Toulouse. Hugh Capet's father had been duke of France and of Burgundy. Hugh had felt obliged to give Burgundy to his younger brother, but he had retained control of its bishoprics and great abbeys. Hugh himself, before he ascended the throne, was duke of France. This duchy included all the land between Flanders and Normandy on the north and Burgundy and Aquitaine on the south—a wide strip of territory running from the tip of the peninsula of Brittany to the frontier of Lorraine. Unfortunately over most of this territory Hugh's power was simply that of a feudal overlord. In Brittany the local counts were practically independent and had obtained control of the episcopal sees and abbeys. In Anjou the viscounts who had ruled as the representatives of the Capetian counts had usurped the title of count and were rapidly securing complete control of the region.

The same situation existed in the counties of Tours,
Blois, Chartres, Meaux, Provins, and several others.
The only counties directly under the control of Hugh
Capet were Paris, Orleans, and Dreux. There lay the
royal manors that supported Hugh and his court and
from there he drew his army. Hugh did, however,
succeed in keeping control of the bishoprics and abbeys outside of Brittany and their resources were perhaps the chief basis of his power.

During the years 987–1108 Hugh Capet, his son,
his grandson, and his great-grandson lost ground steadily before the rising power of their vassals both great
and small. William, duke of Normandy, not only
increased his power enormously by conquering England but he also took away from his Capetian suzerain
the overlordship of Brittany. Two groups of counties
in the duchy of France, Chartres and Blois to the west
of Paris and Meaux and Provins to the east, came into
the hands of a single family that also held the county
of Troyes from the duke of Burgundy. By forcing
the archbishop of Rheims and several other prelates
to grant them a large part of their lands as fiefs and
obliging weak vassals of the crown to become their
vassals the counts of Chartres and Troyes built up a
great feudal state that is usually known as the county
of Champagne. In so doing they deprived the Capetian
kings of a large part of their duchy of France and
caught the royal counties of Paris and Orleans in a vise
between the eastern and western parts of their lands.

The descendants of Hugh Capet found it impossible to control even the minor lords of their counties of Paris and Orleans. Local barons built strong castles in the country around Paris and openly defied the royal power. More than once the king of France met defeat in pitched battle against the barons of the Ile de France. One suffered the deep humiliation of being captured by one of his vassals and being freed by the militia of Paris.

One may well ask how under these circumstances the Capetian monarchy was able to survive. Perhaps the chief reason was that no one had any great interest in overthrowing it. The feudal pyramid needed a head, and the great lords preferred that the holder of the theoretical suzerainty should not be powerful enough to trouble them. Certainly the great vassals of the crown were far too jealous of each other's power to allow one of their number to seize the throne. Then throughout this difficult period the church of France consistently supported the Capetian dynasty. The church was anxious to decrease even if it could not hope to eliminate the almost continual feudal warfare that wasted the realm, and the chief hope of doing this seemed to lie in the development of the royal authority. Thus, although several of the Capetian kings quarreled bitterly with the church and even suffered excommunication, they could rely on the support of the ecclesiastical lords against their lay vassals. Moreover, the church preached the sanctity of the royal office and the king's person. Feudal theory itself gave a certain sanctity to the person and family of the suzerain. In short, the Capetians were not powerful enough to give their vassals much trouble and their demesnes were not great enough to arouse much greed. It was not worth while to attempt to crush the anointed sovereign and feudal suzerain for the slight benefits that might be gained from such an act.

The Increase of Royal Power

In the year 1108 Louis VI succeeded his father Philip I, the great-grandson of Hugh Capet, on the French throne. With his accession began a period of two hundred years in which the royal power steadily increased. This development was made possible by many diverse circumstances. Of the seven kings who reigned during this period four were men of high competence and only one was definitely ineffective. Thus in general the Capetian monarchs had the ability required to make the most of favorable conditions. Sometimes the circumstances that aided the monarchy were purely fortuitous—the weakness of character of a great vassal or the death of one without a male heir. But far more important than the capacity to make the most of sudden strokes of good fortune was the continuing ability of the French kings to use for their benefit fundamental changes in the civilization of western Europe. Hence, before examining in detail the process by which the monarchy increased in power, it seems well to glance at these fundamental changes as they effected political institutions.

Certain vital changes in the economic structure of western Europe that took place in the eleventh, twelfth, and thirteenth centuries have been discussed in an earlier volume in this series. Here we are interested in them only as they affected the political balance of power. The great reclamation movement that put into cultivation vast areas of wasteland, marsh, and forest benefited the entire feudal hierarchy. Every lord who founded new villages increased his resources in produce and labor. But in general the great lords profited far more than their vassals because the extensive forests and vast tracts of waste and marsh were usually in their demesnes. Thus the large-scale clearings in the forest of Rennes benefited the duke of Brittany and his chief vassal, the lord of Vitré, the latter having a share only because he was the duke's brother-in-law. The forest of Rennes had been ducal demesne. The Capetian kings as dukes of France made full use of this movement. On the route between Paris and Orleans and in its immediate vicinity nine new royal settlements appeared during the twelfth century. The great forests that surrounded Paris were reduced to isolated fragments little larger than they are today.

Of far greater significance than the bringing of new land into cultivation were the development of commerce, the growth of towns, and the reappearance of a money economy. Once more all the members of the feudal hierarchy profited to some extent, but the advantages of the higher lords over the lower ones became greater. The simple knight or petty baron might collect tolls in money from merchants traveling through his lands, might sponsor and reap the profits from a small local fair, and might have a small town in his possession. But the management of great fairs such as those of Champagne and the possession of important centers of commerce fell to the great lords like the counts of Flanders and Champagne and the dukes of Normandy. Here again the Capetian kings as dukes of France took full advantage of their opportunities. They scattered chartered towns over their demesnes and ringed Paris with prosperous fairs.

Money Revenues

The possession of revenues in money very greatly strengthened the position of a feudal prince. He could hire soldiers to fight for him and was no longer entirely dependent on the military service of his vassals. These soldiers would fight, as long as they were paid, against any enemy of their employer. No longer could a contumacious vassal escape punishment simply because his fellow vassals were unwilling to aid the lord against him. No longer could a rebellious baron shut himself up in his castle with the assurance that he was safe because the reduction of his fortress would require more than the forty days that the feudal levy would serve. Obviously this change in the position of the feudal princes was very gradual as was the development of their sources of money revenues. By the late twelfth century the duke of Normandy, the duke of France, or the count of Flanders could reduce the castle of a rebellious vassal with hired troops, but it was very expensive and took a large part of his available resources. He did this only when the need was very great. A century later a feat of this sort was by no means such a serious matter.

The feudal prince could not only hire soldiers—he could also hire officials. His agents need no longer be his vassals whose primary interests were like those of their fellow vassals. He could employ officers who would make the development of his power their chief concern. These officers did not have to be knights who were steeped in feudal ideas. The rising merchant class provided men with a different point of view and little interest in the privileges and power of the feudal class.

It is important to remember that these economic changes benefited all the great lords. The duke of Normandy and the counts of Flanders and Champagne profited from them fully as much as did the Capetian king as duke of France. These general conditions enabled the king to build up his power in his own demesne, but as we shall see it was largely a marvelous combination of skill and good luck that enabled him to increase that demesne at the expense of his great vassals.

The Reformed and Revived Papacy

During the eleventh and twelfth centuries one important new element that was not economic in origin

was introduced into the politics of western Europe—
the reformed and revived papacy. As we have seen,
the royal power in the ninth, tenth, and early eleventh
centuries had leaned heavily on a close alliance with
the church. The king was both a secular and ecclesiastical dignitary. He controlled the personnel and the
resources of the church within his realm. But the re-
invigorated papacy was anxious to develop its own
control over the church as a whole. It was unwilling
to have kings appoint prelates as they saw fit. The
popes even claimed that they could depose kings who
violated the laws of the church. They denied that the
kings were priestly in character—that the kingship
was a sacred office. To popes like Gregory VII a king
was a sort of police captain dependent on the papal
power. Now this new view was not universally accepted by the churchmen of Europe. In fact there was
a strong tendency for the ecclesiastics of each realm
to support their monarch as they had in the past. But
the papacy did vastly increase its power and become a
vital factor in the secular politics of western Europe.
And it was strongly inclined to use its power to weaken
the great monarchies.

This new papal policy was one of the chief causes
of the destruction of the German monarchy and at
times hampered severely the development of the royal
power in England, but the Capetians were far more
fortunate than their rivals. During the first great struggle between the pope and the kings—the investiture

controversy—the attention of the papacy was centered on Germany. The French kings had a few skirmishes with the papacy, but they were of minor importance. Later when the popes sought to gain their ends by active participation in secular politics, the Capetians succeeded in being their allies at all the crucial moments. When at last, in the late thirteenth century, the papacy turned its face from the prostrate German monarchy to throw its full power against the Capetians, the latter were powerful enough to win the struggle.

The Pacification of the Demesne

Louis VI was extremely vigorous both mentally and physically. Although as he advanced in years his enormous size made it very difficult to find a horse that could carry him, he continued to lead his troops about his realm. He came to the throne determined to crush the turbulent petty lords of the duchy of France and to do what he could to strengthen his authority outside his demesne. In both these enterprises he had an invaluable ally—Suger, abbot of St. Denis. St. Denis was one of the greatest of French monasteries. The king himself was its advocate and its vassal for the region called the Vexin that lay on the frontier between the duchy of France and Normandy. The traditional banner of the French kings, the oriflamme, was the standard of St. Denis, borne by them as its advocates. Louis had studied in the monastic school at St. Denis and

there had met Suger. The royal influence rapidly
raised Suger to the abbacy. He was the ideal prime
minister for a mediaeval monarch. On the one hand,
he was completely devoted to the development of the
royal power and was ready to support the king against
all rivals whether secular or ecclesiastical. At the same
time his private life and his administration of his abbey
earned him the respect of the most rigid prelates.
Even his bitter political foe, the great St. Bernard of
Clairvaux, admired the sanctity of his life and character.

Backed by both the spiritual and temporal support
of the bishops and abbots of his demesne, Louis waged
ceaseless war against the barons of his duchy. His usual
practice was to summon a baron to appear before his
feudal court to answer the charges of the people he
had plundered, imprisoned, and maimed. When the
baron failed to appear, he was declared contumacious.
Before marching against the rebel, Louis would further
strengthen his hand by having his foe solemnly excommunicated. The reduction of a powerful baron was
not easy. For seven years the king waged war against
Hugh de Puiset. Time after time he razed Hugh's chief
castle, but each time the baron managed to rebuild it.
Finally Hugh was crushed and deprived of his fief.
The resistance of Thomas de Marly was even more
stubborn. This fierce lord, who was the terror of the
countryside and a lecherous, sadistic enemy of all
mankind, maintained his position for sixteen years

of troops and forced the usurper to withdraw. In 1122 the bishop of Clermont was driven from his lands and even his episcopal city by the count of Auvergne. Although no king of France for many years had attempted to exercise his authority so far from Paris, Louis marched into Auvergne and restored the bishop. Five years later the count of Flanders was murdered by a band of assassins. Louis entered Flanders, punished the criminals, and installed as count his friend and ally William, son of Robert of Normandy. As William was quickly driven out by the rightful heir to the county, Louis' intervention cannot be called a complete success, but he had shown his determination to exercise his rights as feudal suzerain. This energetic policy made a great impression on the feudal princes of France. When William X, duke of Aquitaine, lord of the most extensive fief in southern France, felt himself near death, he sent a message to Louis begging the king to care for his only child, his daughter Eleanor, and suggested that she be married to the king's eldest son, Louis.

Eleanor of Aquitaine

Louis VI and Duke William of Aquitaine died within a few months of each other in 1137, and the new king, Louis VII, married Eleanor and became duke of Aquitaine. If one glances at a map, this will seem to mark an enormous increase in the royal power, but actually the possession of Aquitaine was of little

against all the power Louis could muster. But on
one the barons of the Ile de France were reduce
obedience. When Louis died, the king of France
the effective master of his duchy. The descendan
the lords he had curbed were to be his successors'
loyal servants and allies in their struggles agains
great vassals of the crown.

In addition to waging war on the barons of
duchy of France, Louis was frequently force
defend his lands from the attacks of two of his
vassals—Henry I, duke of Normandy and kir
England, and his nephew, Theobald, count of
and Champagne. With Normandy bordering
duchy of France on the northeast, Blois on the
and Champagne on the east, Louis was in an extre
precarious position. Fortunately he could usuall
on the support of the count of Anjou, who wa
position to attack both his foes. Moreover, He
was always faced with a determined oppositi
Normandy led by his brother Robert and the la
son William. Thus by stirring up and encouragir
count of Anjou and Robert's party in Norn
Louis could divert the attention of his two pov
enemies.

Despite his almost continuous campaigns v
and on the frontiers of his duchy of France, Lou
few opportunities to exploit his position as ki
France. In 1109 the uncle of the infant lord of
bon usurped his nephew's fief. Louis gathered a

value to Louis VII. The dukes of Aquitaine had been
the overlords of a vast territory stretching from the
Pyrenees almost to the river Loire and at its widest
point reaching close to the bank of the Rhône. But
most of this area was in the hands of powerful lords
whom the duke was completely unable to control. His
real power lay in a few small districts lying around his
chief seats—Bayonne, Bordeaux, and Poitiers. Even
an energetic and warlike duke who resided in the
duchy could exercise only limited authority. Louis VII
was a gentle, kindly, pious man whose residence was
far away. The ducal demesnes around Bayonne, Bordeaux, and Poitiers were too far away to add much
strength to the royal power, and the great lords of
Aquitaine ignored their new duke as cheerfully as
they had his predecessors and would his successors. A
wife that brought him a barony with a few castles
somewhere near Paris would have been far more valuable to Louis than was Eleanor.

Although Louis VII was a far feebler figure than
his father, the general policy of the Capetian house
remained unchanged. Until his death Suger served
the son as he had the father. The bitter war with the
house of Blois continued. Louis, like his father, wasted
few opportunities to exercise the royal authority. Once
more the bishop of Clermont was supported against
the count of Auvergne. The plundering lord of Polig-
nac was suppressed. When the count of Nevers aided
the people of Vezelay against their lord the abbot,

the crown intervened to settle the dispute. More and more the idea grew that the king was the natural keeper of the peace and protector of the weak—especially of the church. Where bishops or abbots suffered from the depredations of secular lords, they complained to the king's court.

The House of Anjou

During the early years of the reign of Louis VII the foundations were laid for a feudal state that was to threaten the very existence of the Capetian monarchy. In the vain hope of breaking the alliance between Louis VI and Geoffrey, count of Anjou, King Henry I of England had given the count his daughter Matilda in marriage. When Henry died, his nephew Stephen of Blois, younger brother of Count Theobald of Blois and Champagne, seized the English throne. Matilda crossed to England to wage a long civil war against Stephen while her husband Geoffrey attacked Normandy. To have their bitter foes, the house of Blois, hold Normandy would have been a major disaster for the Capetian kings. Hence Louis VII favored the efforts of Count Geoffrey who gradually conquered the duchy in the name of his young son Henry. As soon as Henry was old enough, he himself took over the government of Normandy. In 1151 Geoffrey died and Henry became master of Normandy and Anjou. As the dukes of Normandy were suzerains of Brittany, this gave Henry control of western France from the mouth of the Somme to that of the Loire. The marriage of Louis VII with Eleanor of Aquitaine had never been happy. Eleanor was the granddaughter of William IX of Aquitaine, one of the first troubadors. She was deeply imbued with the spirit of the troubadors and their gay science of love. If one third the contemporary stories about her are true, she was far from prudish in her personal conduct. Louis was solemn, pious, and inclined toward asceticism. But the most serious difficulty was that Eleanor failed to produce a male heir and so threatened the future of the Capetian dynasty. In 1152 a group of French prelates declared the marriage annulled on the customary grounds of consanguinity and before the year was over Eleanor had married young Henry of Normandy and Anjou. Although Henry was never able to control the barons of Aquitaine, his possession of three great fiefs made him an immensely powerful feudal prince. Then in 1153 Henry came to an agreement with King Stephen by which he would succeed to the throne on the latter's death, and in 1154 he became king of England. Thus the most powerful and most dangerous vassal of the French crown had behind him the resources of the English realm.

Louis VII combated this new menace to the French royal power as well as his limited capacities would permit. He waged war against Henry II, but he was no match for his rival as a soldier. Louis was more successful in intrigue. He succeeded in persuading Henry's

eldest son to rebel against his father. As young Prince
Henry was supported by a large number of Anglo-
Norman barons who chafed under the king's heavy-
handed rule, this revolt was a serious threat to
Henry II. If Louis had supported his allies with energy, Henry might have been crushed. But the French
king did little more than raid the Norman frontier
and Henry was able to suppress the revolt. King Louis
fell back on a new series of alliances—he came to terms
with the house of Blois. His eldest daughter Marie
married Henry, count of Champagne, her younger
sister Alice became the wife of Henry's brother, Theobald, count of Blois, while Louis himself married the
counts' sister Adèle. During the last years of his reign
Louis was completely dominated by his strong-minded
brothers-in-law, Henry, count of Champagne, Theobald, count of Blois, and their brother William, archbishop of Rheims.

Philip Augustus

Adèle of Blois bore Louis the much-desired male
heir—Philip, known to history as Philip Augustus.
Philip bore little resemblance to his father. Although
he was never particularly effective as a soldier, he had
all the other qualities needed by a successful monarch
—sagacity, unscrupulousness, and invincible determination to increase the royal authority. When he
reached the age of fifteen, he found the sight of his
doddering old father in the tutelage of the house of

Blois completely unbearable. Philip gathered support by marrying the niece of the count of Flanders and forming an alliance with Henry II. By this means he was enabled to drive his uncles from power, and he was the effective master of the realm some months before his father died.

Although he had used an alliance with Henry II to enable him to escape from the dominance of the house of Blois, Philip fully realized that the Angevin kings of England were the chief threat to the Capetian monarchy, and he devoted the major part of his life to breaking their power. He started by following his father's policy of stirring up Henry's sons against him. When Henry died at Chinon in 1189, his two surviving legitimate sons, Richard and John, were in rebellion against him in alliance with Philip. But the French king gained little by this maneuver. Richard was an abler soldier than his father and equally determined to defend his fiefs from King Philip. In 1190 Richard and Philip left together on a crusade. But while they were waging war in Palestine, Philip learned of the death of the count of Flanders and hastened home to make good his young son's rights to his mother's share of the inheritance. The new count of Flanders was forced to surrender the rich county of Artois to Philip to hold as guardian for his son Louis. Then Philip proceeded to see what he could do about seizing Richard's lands while he was still in Palestine. His first step was to confer with the seneschal of Normandy, who ruled the duchy in Richard's absence, and show him a treaty supposed to have been agreed to by Richard that gave the French king a fair part of the duchy. As the seneschal felt certain that Richard would not have made such an agreement, he refused to honor it. Philip's answer was to summon his host for the invasion of Normandy. But an attack on the lands of a crusader was a serious offense involving immediate excommunication, and Philip's vassals refused to follow him. The king then tried another device—intriguing with Richard's younger brother John. Soon he had a close alliance with that fickle prince. News of all this reached Richard in Palestine and he hurried home. On the way he had the misfortune to be captured by a German lord, who turned him over to his enemy, the Emperor Henry VI. Philip promptly offered the emperor a large sum of money to keep Richard in prison. Unfortunately for Philip's plans, the princes of Germany forced the emperor to accept the ransom offered by the English government. After he was freed, Richard waged bitter war with Philip for the rest of his life.

King John

Richard was killed while besieging the castle of one of his Poitevin vassals in 1199 and was succeeded by his brother John. The new king was not so able a warrior as his brother. Moreover, he made two serious mistakes. The feudal power of the county of

Poitou was divided between two great houses—the Lusignans who held the county of La Marche and the counts of Angoulême. The count of Angoulême had affianced his daughter and heiress to the count of La Marche. This alarmed John. He marched into Poitou and persuaded the count of Angoulême to let him marry the girl. To steal the fiancée of one's vassal was a serious violation of feudal custom. The whole Lusignan family rose in revolt and appealed to John's overlord, Philip, for justice. When John refused to appear before Philip's court to answer for his offense, he was solemnly declared contumacious and deprived of all the fiefs he held of the French crown. But this declaration was of little practical value—John had to be driven out. His next mistake helped Philip to do that. John had been the fourth son of Henry II. His elder brother Geoffrey, who had been married to the heiress of Brittany, had died leaving a son named Arthur. At the time Richard died, Arthur was a young boy who had spent much of his youth in King Philip's court. Hence the Anglo-Norman barons had preferred to have John as their king, and Arthur became count of Anjou and duke of Brittany as a vassal of John. When Philip's court declared John's fiefs forfeited, the French king gave Arthur some troops and sent him into Anjou to wage war against his uncle. In the summer of 1203 he was captured by John and imprisoned in the castle of Falaise. He was never seen alive again, and there is strong reason for believing that John had him murdered. The disappearance of their young lord enraged the barons of Anjou and Brittany and they immediately went over to King Philip. The barons of England had no great interest in the defense of Normandy and very little confidence in John. By a discreet mixture of force and well-placed bribes Philip quickly conquered the duchy. Normandy and Anjou were added to the Capetian demesne. Arthur's young half sister was married to a cousin of King Philip, Peter of Dreux, and Brittany placed in apparently reliable hands.

The Battle of Bouvines

John had no intention of giving up Normandy and Anjou without making an effort to recover them. He promptly set about raising a war chest in England through heavy taxation. He also built up a system of alliances on the continent. The German emperor, Otto of Brunswick, was John's nephew. Large sums of money went from England to buy the support of the German princes. Then John succeeded in forming an alliance with two of Philip's vassals, the counts of Flanders and Boulogne. The English king had an excellent plan. Otto, the counts of Flanders and Boulogne, and the German princes were to march against Paris from the north. He himself would land in Poitou with an army and attack from the south. The French king would be caught in a vise and completely crushed.

This was the great crisis of Philip's reign. Fortunately for him John moved too slowly and was still on the borders of Anjou when Otto moved against Paris. Philip met Otto and completely defeated him in the great battle of Bouvines, and John was forced to make a truce and retire to England. Philip had won the contest against the house of Anjou. John's successors were to make many attempts to reconquer all or part of their ancient fiefs in France, yet not until the middle of the fourteenth century were these efforts to be seriously dangerous to the French crown. The English kings remained in possession of Bordeaux and Bayonne, but Normandy, Anjou, and a large part of Aquitaine came into the hands of the Capetians.

Although Artois, Normandy, and Anjou were the chief additions made to the royal demesne by Philip Augustus, the foundation for another accretion was laid during his reign. The great county of Toulouse in southern France had become one of the chief centers of the Albigensian heresy. The count of Toulouse and his barons were not heretics, but they sympathized with them and made no effort to support the church's attempts to suppress them. The strained relations between the count and the church reached the breaking point when a papal legate was slain by one of the count's retainers. Pope Innocent III preached a crusade against the count and the heretics of his lands and called on King Philip to lead it. The king had no desire to place himself in the peculiar position of attacking a vassal under these circumstances. The great lords of northern France were equally disinclined to be involved in the affair. But Simon de Montfort, whose ancestral lands lay on the borders between France and Normandy and who had lost most of them by being squeezed between John and Philip, undertook the adventure. Supported by knights who sought salvation and profit, Simon conquered Toulouse and was installed as count by the pope. His son Amaury found himself unable to maintain his position and surrendered the great fief to the French crown.

When Philip died in 1223, the French crown was triumphant over its great vassals. Artois, Normandy, and Anjou were part of the royal demesne. The count of Flanders, captured at Bouvines, lay in a royal prison. The effective authority of the English kings in their duchy of Aquitaine was reduced to the environs of Bordeaux and Bayonne. The count of Toulouse was a baron from the Île de France who depended entirely on troops and money from northern France. Of the six great secular vassals of the French crown only the duke of Burgundy and the count of Champagne still maintained their position. Philip had at least tripled the size and resources of the royal demesne and had broken the power of the feudal princes.

The Royal Administration

The demesne of Philip Augustus required far more administrative machinery than had the small duchy of

France. The government of the early Capetian kings had been extremely simple. The officers of the king's household had also managed the affairs of state. The seneschal who had the responsibility for feeding and clothing the court had general supervision over the demesne that supplied the necessary resources. The constable and the marshal cared for the king's horses and commanded his troops in battle. When the king needed advice, these household officers and such vassals as happened to be on hand supplied it. When a case was brought before the king's court, a similar group heard and decided it. The king's interests in the various royal estates were looked after by hereditary officials called provosts, who paid the crown a fixed sum every year and kept whatever else they could collect. As a rule these payments were probably in kind. The king and his court moved about the demesne eating the produce of his estates.

The expansion of the business of the royal court in the reigns of Louis VI and Louis VII brought a new element into the administration, composed usually of clerks in minor orders who had been trained in the law. They sat with the officers of the household and the vassals of the duchy of France in hearing cases of importance, and many lesser cases were probably handled by the clerks alone. These new men were of middle-class origin, and their chief interest was to serve their master the king.

When he increased the extent of his demesne, Philip

Augustus had no desire to appoint additional hereditary provosts. Instead he divided the new territory into
districts and placed middle-class administrators called
baillis in charge of them. These *baillis* were removable
at the king's will, and he changed their districts frequently to prevent them from becoming settled in
power. They were expected to pay over everything
they collected and in turn received a salary. In certain
districts these bourgeois officials could not be used
successfully. The soldiers of the day being generally
disinclined to obey anyone who was not a knight, it
was necessary for the king to have noble agents in regions that required strong garrison forces. Hence the
country bordering the duchy of Aquitaine was ruled
by seneschals of knightly rank. Both the *baillis* and
the seneschals had subordinate officials who aided
them in administering their charges. In this way the
French crown developed a hierarchy of paid civil
servants who were devoted to the interests of the
king.

Philip Augustus left the Capetian monarchy firmly
established. The next four generations of French kings
simply built a rather more imposing structure on the
foundations he had laid. It would not be practical to
follow their careers in detail, but it is necessary to
examine certain important aspects of the history of
France during the century following Philip's death.

Royal Appanages

Philip's son and successor Louis VIII made one important innovation—he started the so-called appanage system to care for his younger sons. This problem of how to support the king's younger sons had troubled the early Capetians very little. Robert, the second Capetian king, had given the duchy of Burgundy to his second son. His successor, Henry I, had married his second son to a rich heiress. Louis VI had used the same device to care for his sons Robert and Peter. No one of these had received any material part of the royal demesne. But Louis VIII had a number of sons to care for and he assigned them important parts of his demesne. One was given Artois, another Anjou, and a third Poitou. This policy has been severely criticized by historians. The royal demesne that had been built up with so much labor was parceled out once more. A king might be able to rely on his brothers, but could his son trust his cousins or his grandson his second cousins? Actually it seems likely that Louis was merely being realistic. No thirteenth-century government could rule effectively too extended a territory. If they were to be loyal and reasonably honest, the *baillis* and seneschals needed continual supervision. A count of the royal house actually resident in the district was the best way of supplying this supervision.

Nor did the practice of giving appanages permanently diminish the royal demesne. The county of

Toulouse came into the hands of the crown under the successors of Philip Augustus; and somewhat later Champagne suffered the same fate. The grandson of Louis VIII married the heiress of Champagne and so brought that great fief into the royal demesne. By the end of the thirteenth century all that remained of the six great fiefs once held directly of the crown were the county of Flanders, the duchy of Burgundy, and the remnants of the duchy of Aquitaine. In their place were a number of smaller fiefs held by the cadet branches of the Capetian house—the counties of Artois, Anjou, and Valois and the lordship of Bourbon. The crown steadily encroached on the independence of all the great lords. Feudal custom had always provided that when a lord refused to hear a vassal's case in his court, the latter could appeal to the overlord. Philip's grandson, Louis IX, commonly called St. Louis, maintained that the vassal could appeal if he considered the decision unjust. This opened all the great fiefs to the king's judges and officials. The kings also denied their vassals the right to participate in the election of bishops. Only one fief escaped from this tightening royal control. The Capetian dukes of Brittany, descended from Peter of Dreux, had built up the ducal power and developed an effective feudal state. They were strong enough to defy the kings. No case could be appealed from the duke's court to the king's, no royal official could enter Brittany without the duke's leave, and the duke controlled his ecclesiastical benefices as the king did his. In short, Brittany became practically an independent state bound to France only by its duke's homage to the king.

The Royal Administration of Justice

St. Louis and his successors devoted much of their attention to checking the chief curse of most feudal states—private warfare among the nobles. St. Louis hedged private war about with complicated rules that took most of the fun out of it. Before attacking your neighbor you had to give him notice, and you had to ask his relatives whether or not they wanted to be included in the war. If your enemy asked for a truce, you had to grant it. You could not slaughter your foe's peasants or burn their crops. Royal officials stood ready to enforce these rules. Louis' grandson, Philip IV, went even farther. He forbade private war and made it illegal for the nobles to ride about armed. But this was too serious an attack on the privileges of the feudal class and his sons were obliged to abandon this legislation.

During the century following the death of Philip Augustus the French royal administration developed steadily. The little band of professional jurists that had served King Philip grew into the *Parlement* of Paris, the supreme court of the realm. Most routine cases were handled by these professional judges. Only when noblemen of importance were involved were vassals of the crown called upon to reinforce the court. The

royal administration also developed a financial branch,
the *chambre des comptes*. This body received the
money due to the king from *baillis* and provosts and
kept account of its expenditure. The money revenues
of the crown had grown enormously. Philip Augustus
had supported his government from feudal obligations, such as reliefs, and from the revenues of his demesne. St. Louis collected regular taxes. They were
for the most part income and property taxes levied on
the realm as a whole. Usually the king admitted that
he could not collect these taxes in the lands of the great
lords without their consent. A common device was
to offer to split the proceeds between king and lord. In
short, by the end of the thirteenth century the Capetian monarchy had a comparatively well-developed
central administration supported by taxation as well
as the traditional revenues.

The Church and the State

The relations between crown and church provide
a particularly interesting feature of this period. One
issue was the ancient question of episcopal elections.
According to the compromise reached in the twelfth
century, the cathedral chapters elected the bishop in
the presence of the king or his agent. Obviously, unless
the king's candidate was outrageously unsuitable, he
was elected without any dispute. Then in the thirteenth century the popes began to claim that unless
the election by the chapter was unanimous, they had

the final decision. To all intents and purposes this ended the elective power of the chapters and bishops were appointed by the pope. Usually he appointed the royal nominee, but he could always use his power for political bargaining. Another issue was the king's right to tax the clergy and the estates of the church. The kings maintained that the clergy should bear their share of the cost of defending the realm, but the papacy insisted that churchmen could not be taxed without its consent. Here too the matter was usually compromised—the pope gave his consent in return for a *quid pro quo*, often a share of the proceeds.

Shortly after the middle of the thirteenth century the papacy had broken the last fragments of the power of the German emperors in Italy—in fact, with the assistance of other circumstances, it had destroyed the German monarchy. It was almost inevitable that sooner or later a conflict would break out between the triumphant papacy and the dominant power of western Europe, the great Capetian monarchy. In 1294 the cardinals elected to the papal throne an arrogant, ambitious, and determined prelate who took the name of Boniface VIII. The crown of France was worn by Philip IV, who was just as arrogant, just as determined, and far more unscrupulous. Soon king and pope were at bitter feud. The quarrel started with Philip's efforts to remove a bishop. But soon the pope struck at a vital point—the royal power to tax the church. In the bull *Clericis laicos* he absolutely forbade any secular power to tax the clergy without papal consent. Philip replied by stopping all the papal revenues from France. The quarrel was patched up only to break out again in a still more virulent form. An agent of King Philip allied with Roman enemies of Boniface and actually kidnaped the pope. Although he was soon rescued, he died shortly after. Then Philip centered all his power and influence on gaining control of the papacy. In 1305 his partisans elected as pope the archbishop of Bordeaux. The new pope, Clement V, moved the papal court to Avignon, appointed enough French cardinals to give Philip control of the college, and in general obeyed the mandates of the man to whom he owed the papal throne.

The Estates General

The struggle with the papacy led to the creation of a new French political institution—the Estates General. Philip felt the need of showing the pope and the world in general that he had the firm support of his people. Hence, in 1302 he summoned a meeting of representatives of the estates of his realm—nobles, clergy, and townsmen. They gave full support to the king's policy toward the papacy. Philip then decided that this body could be useful for other purposes as well. As will become even more clearly apparent in the case of the English monarchy, the theory of feudal monarchy did not permit a king to levy general taxes without securing the approval of his people in some form. Philip's predecessors had used different devices—meetings of representatives of nobles and clergy, bargains with towns, and gatherings of local or provincial estates. The Estates General gave the crown the machinery necessary to do this on a national basis. Thus the Estates General was invented by the king for his own convenience and to strengthen his power. It seems obvious to us that such an institution might become a means of controlling the king, but it is unlikely that such a possibility occurred to Philip. Getting a tax levy always involved a good deal of argument and negotiation with nobles, clergy, and townsmen; through the Estates General it could all be done at once.

The reign of Philip IV saw the French feudal monarchy at its apex. With the exception of the duke of Brittany and the duke of Gascony the great vassals of the crown were definitely under the royal authority. Cases from their courts were appealed to the *Parlement* at Paris and royal officers freely entered their lands. The lesser nobility had lost their right to private war and were limited in their right to bear arms. The monarchy had developed a complex bureaucracy. Professional financial officers in the *chambre des comptes* saw to the king's finances and professional jurists manned his courts. His *baillis* and their deputies were scattered over the realm. When the king needed an official expression of his people's support either for his policy or for a tax levy, he could summon an Estates

General. Philip was far from an absolute monarch—no king could be absolute whose right to rule was largely based on his position as feudal suzerain and hence was bound by feudal custom. But some of Philip's servants who had studied Roman law thought of the royal power as similar to that of the Roman emperor and did their best to make that conception a reality. The seeds of the later French monarchy existed in Philip's reign.

CHAPTER II

England 〰〰〰〰〰〰〰

THE Anglo-Saxon state of the tenth and eleventh centuries was a Germanic monarchy. The kingship was elective in the ancient royal house of Wessex. An assembly of lay and ecclesiastical magnates, the Witan, elected the king and served as his council. The king had the right to demand military service from every able-bodied man. He also had a group of men called thanes who held land in return for serving him as soldiers—a system somewhat like that of the Carolingian *vassi dominici*. The king and his court were supported by demesne manors scattered over England. During the Viking invasions of the eighth and ninth centuries the English kings had levied a general tax called danegeld to buy off the invaders, and in the eleventh century the Danish conqueror, Canute, used this tax to support his army of occupation. While there is some doubt that an English king could rightfully levy this tax in peacetime, there existed a system of assessment based on land and its value. The king had close control over the church and chose its prelates as he saw fit. He could also, with the approval of the Witan, issue decrees that had the force of law. But the administration of justice was carried on in local popular courts according to ancient custom. These courts, which administered both secular and ecclesiastical law, were presided over by three officials—the bishop, the earl, and the sheriff. The earl was the chief local officer and was chosen by the king with the approval of the Witan. The sheriff was the king's personal representative who administered his demesne manors and collected his dues of every sort.

The Elements of Feudalism

Anglo-Saxon England had certain basic elements of feudalism similar to those that had existed in the early Carolingian state. Royal thanes held land in return for military service and many great landholders had their own thanes who held from them on the same basis. It is quite possible that given the necessary conditions the Anglo-Saxon state would have in time become feudalized without outside interference. But it never had time to develop to that point. In 1066 William, duke of Normandy, invaded England, defeated and killed King Harold, and subdued the whole country. William had been brought up in a feudal environment, was the head of a great French fief, and was followed to England by men who were equally imbued with feudal ideas. Such conquerors could hardly fail to turn England into a feudal state. But William was fully aware that an Anglo-Saxon king had possessed many powers denied to a mere feudal suzerain, and he had every intention of making the most of his position as the lawful successor to Edward the Confessor and Harold. One may even wonder whether William's knowledge of the Capetian monarchy was not enough to make him wary of too pure a feudal structure.

Although King William's basic ideas would probably have led him to establish a feudal state, the military needs of his new kingdom actually left him with little choice. He had to provide a system that would prevent or suppress Saxon risings and safeguard the realm from its external foes. Frontier defenses had to be planned against the Scots and the Welsh. But far more serious was the danger of renewed Scandinavian invasions. To the historian it seems fairly clear that the age of Scandinavian expansion was over by 1066. William had, however, no way of knowing this. In 1013–1017 the Danes had almost conquered England and Canute, king of Denmark, had ruled England for eighteen years. Just before the battle of Hastings King Harold had defeated a Norwegian army at Stamford Bridge. In William's mind the Scandinavian kingdoms were a perpetual menace to his new realm. England needed a network of strong fortresses with men to garrison them and a large field army that could be mustered in time of need. It is probable that under the economic circumstances of the time nothing but a strong feudal system could fill this need. Certainly this was the solution that would occur to William.

The Norman Fiefs

The actual process of dividing England into fiefs must have presented grave difficulties. William and his followers knew little or nothing about the geography of England and had no means of learning much more. There were no registers of lands. William had two methods at his disposal. He could use the established Anglo-Saxon territorial divisions and base his fiefs on them, or he could utilize the existing landholdings and grant as a fief the property of a particular Saxon. The first of these methods would result in integrated territorial fiefs. As the Anglo-Saxon landholders had their possessions widely scattered and intermingled, the use of the second method would avoid compact fiefs. William chose to use both methods. In regions that were of vital strategic importance he granted compact fiefs based on the Anglo-Saxon territorial divisions. The easiest path from Scotland into England lay through Northumbria. Hence the whole shire of Northumberland was granted as a fief to a Norman lord. On the Welsh border the shires of Cheshire, Shropshire, and Herefordshire were handled in the same way. The whole county of Kent was given to William's half brother, the bishop of Bayeux. In Sussex each subdivision or rape was granted to a Norman lord. But throughout the rest of England the Con-

queror's followers received the lands of particular
Saxons and so had their estates scattered and intermingled with those of others.

When King William granted a fief, he evaluated it
as well as he could and set the number of knights that
it was to supply for his feudal host. The few Anglo-
Saxon landholders who were left in possession were
assigned quotas of knights, as were the bishoprics and
abbeys of the realm. The total number of knights provided for seems to have been about 5000. Then in each
important royal borough William built a castle—
either a massive stone tower or a fortified earthen
mound. The command of each castle was entrusted to
a vassal whose lands lay nearby and the garrisons were
supplied by designated fiefs. Moreover, each royal
vassal was encouraged if not actually directed to build
castles and to garrison them with his knights. Thus
there sprang up a vast network of castles. Once this
system was set up and the castles built, England was
comparatively safe from either Saxon revolt or invasion from outside.

The Obligations of the Barons

The men to whom the king granted fiefs are usually
called barons. Each baron owed the king the service
of the number of knights assigned to his fief and all
the ordinary obligations of a vassal to his lord. Each
baron was faced with the problem of providing his
quota of knights. He had two possible alternatives—

either to keep the necessary number of knights in his household ready for service and feed and clothe them from the produce of his estates or to grant fiefs to knights who would serve him. The really great baron who owed 100 knights had little choice—it would be impracticable to keep so great a number in his household. The lesser lord who owed only ten knights might avoid granting fiefs. But here again the ideas of the day had their effect. Every knight wanted a fief of his own, and the lords could not resist the pressure. Hence the barons granted fiefs to men who became their vassals and the king's rear vassals. Sometimes these rear vassals had large fiefs owing ten or more knights, and they in turn granted fiefs to other knights. A feudal hierarchy rapidly developed. The king of England, like the Capetian monarch, was a feudal suzerain who was the apex of a pyramid of lords and vassals. The king had his feudal court, the *curia regis*, consisting of the prelates and barons of the realm. Each baron also had his court where his vassals met. While the feudal relations between king and barons were decided in the *curia regis*, the relations between a baron and his vassals were worked out in the baron's court. These various feudal courts slowly forged the feudal customs of England.

The Royal Authority

In addition to constructing a feudal hierarchy with himself at its head, William took over the royal heritage of the Anglo-Saxon kings. Although he made an important concession to the church by separating the lay and ecclesiastical courts and allowing the church to set up its legal system as it had in the rest of western Europe, he controlled as closely as had his predecessors the election of bishops and abbots and refused to allow papal legates to enter the realm without his leave. He continued to regard the bishops as part of his administration, and his writs were always addressed to the bishop and the sheriff except in the few shires where he established earls. William recognized fully the value of the right to collect general taxes implicit in the danegeld, and he collected this tax. He was thus the only feudal monarch of western Europe to have financial resources that were entirely nonfeudal in nature. Moreover, King William tried to solve the basic contradiction that existed in a feudal monarchy —that between the conception of a feudal hierarchy in which the suzerain had rights only over his direct vassals and the idea of a monarch and his subjects. He insisted that every freeman, no matter what his feudal position, should swear allegiance to him. Rear vassals of importance also swore fidelity and did homage to the king. Thus in theory at least the obligations of a vassal to his lord were always secondary to his obligations to the king. In France, when a great vassal waged war on the king, he might be committing an offense, but his men who followed him were only doing their duty. In England, any man of any station who bore arms against the king violated his oath and was a traitor.

It was inevitable that neither the successors of King William nor their barons would be willing to keep static the arrangements established by him. Both crown and baronage were bound to attempt to increase their power at the expense of the other. Moreover, both were inclined to usurp the functions and revenues of the popular courts. This struggle between king and barons was the central thread of the political history of England for several centuries.

Feudal Revolt

Comparatively little is known of the progress of this contest during the reigns of William I and William II. There was a serious baronial revolt against the Conqueror and contemporary documents suggest that it was caused by the encroachments of the sheriffs on what the barons considered their privileges. It is clear that both kings made the most of their rights as feudal suzerains. When a baron died, the relief for his fief was set at the highest figure there was any chance of collecting. When a baron wanted to marry his daughter, the king charged a fee for his permission. When a baron died leaving an unmarried heiress, she was sold to the highest bidder. At the same time the great lords had been increasing their power at the expense of the popular courts and the sheriffs. In Anglo-Saxon times most men of importance had had sac and soc—that is, police-court authority over the peasants on their own estates. Many landowners had also had the right called *infangentheof*—the privilege of hanging one of their own men caught red-handed in larceny. Every Norman baron and many of their vassals had these privileges. Then the Anglo-Saxon kings had occasionally given a landholder the revenues from a local or hundred court. Their Norman successors simply absorbed the court and conducted it through their own officers. The Anglo-Saxons had also had a system called frankpledge by which twelve men were bound by oath to produce any one of their number who committed a crime. It was the duty of the sheriff to see that every man in England was in this system, but most great Norman lords had secured or usurped this privilege for themselves. In fact the most powerful of the barons seem to have had the right to forbid the sheriff to enter their lands. His functions on their estates were performed by their own officers. Moreover, the feudal courts had by their very existence taken away much business from the popular courts. In general all civil disputes between vassals of the same lord went to his court.

William the Conqueror divided his lands between his two elder sons. Robert, the eldest, became duke of Normandy, while the next younger, William, received the English crown. The third son, Henry, was given a modest appanage in Normandy. But when King William II was killed while hunting, Henry was in England and hence in a position to seize the throne before Robert could move. He succeeded in persuading the barons of England to accept him as their king—at the cost of a charter of liberties in which he promised to abandon the objectionable practices of his father and brother. Henry would ask only a "reasonable" relief when a baron was succeeded by his heir. He would not take a fee for granting a baron leave to give his daughter in marriage. No widow of a baron would be obliged to marry again against her will. Henry even promised not to collect danegeld from the demesnes of men who held fiefs by knight service—a concession that would have reduced enormously the yield of the levy. But there is no evidence that any of these promises ever troubled King Henry. He seems to have followed consistently the aggressive policies of his father William I and brother William II with improvements of his own devising.

The Royal Officials

William I and William II had in general used great barons as sheriffs and constables of royal castles. This practice had one advantage—the authority of these officials was supported by their own feudal resources as well as by the royal power. But magnates in office were likely to be independent and to favor their fellow barons. Henry tended to choose his officials from the lower feudal ranks and thus acquired servants whose position depended on his continued favor. The

chief of Henry's administration, his justiciar Ralph
Basset, was drawn from that class. King Henry also
developed a group of royal officials who operated his
central administration. Under the Anglo-Saxon kings
certain serious crimes, such as murder, rape, and arson,
were considered offenses against the king. The culprit would be tried in the popular courts, but the king
would set the penalty. William I and William II removed the trial of such cases from the popular courts
and had them heard by royal justices—usually the
sheriff of the county. Henry I sent groups of justices
through the shires to hear these pleas of the crown and
to supervise the conduct of the sheriffs and other local
officials. He also established an efficient financial system. His treasurer, Nigel, bishop of Ely, organized the
exchequer. Here the sheriffs and others who owed
the crown money appeared to pay their obligations
and render their accounts before a group of royal
officials—the barons of the exchequer. These various
functions were all carried out by the same group of
men. The same men were the king's justices, the barons
of the exchequer, and often served as sheriffs and constables. The justiciar was their chief. When the king
was in Normandy, the justiciar ruled England as his
viceroy.

Henry I ruled England with a heavy hand. He not
only made the most of his feudal rights such as relief,
wardship, and marriage, but he also prevented his
barons from usurping rights of jurisdiction and for-

bade them to build castles without his permission. The
barons were inclined to look longingly toward Normandy where pleasant anarchy reigned under the mild
and ineffective rule of Duke Robert. The result was a
series of revolts against Henry by supporters of his
brother. Henry crushed the risings, invaded Normandy, subdued the duchy, and captured his brother,
who died years later in an English prison. A large part
of the rest of Henry's reign was occupied in trying to
bring the turbulent Norman baronage to order and
in waging war against his Capetian overlord and his
ally the count of Anjou. In all these contests Henry
emerged triumphant, but fate dealt him a crushing
blow. His only legitimate son was drowned crossing
from Normandy to England. Henry obliged his prelates and barons to swear to accept as his heir his daughter Matilda, widow of the Emperor Henry V and wife
of Count Geoffrey of Anjou. But he probably realized
that when he died his barons would be inclined to seek
a mild and weak monarch rather than the stern and
able Matilda and her fierce Angevin husband. There
was such a candidate for the throne: Henry's sister
had married Count Stephen of Blois, and although
their eldest son Theobald was fully as formidable as
his uncle, his younger brother Stephen, whom King
Henry had endowed with vast lands in England and
Normandy, was noted for his mildness. And many
men doubted that it was proper for a woman to in-
herit the kingdom of England.

Feudal Anarchy

When Henry died in 1135, his nephew Stephen promptly crossed to England and was accepted as king by the prelates and barons of the realm. Count Theobald of Blois occupied Normandy but soon relinquished it to his brother. Count Geoffrey of Anjou and Matilda refused to accept this arrangement. Geoffrey invaded Normandy while Matilda crossed to England to attempt to wrest the throne from Stephen. The result was a long and bitter civil war that brought England to a state of almost complete anarchy. The barons supported whichever side promised them the most extensive privileges. Moreover, the general state of confusion made usurpation easy. If a baron could persuade neither Stephen nor Matilda to allow him to build castles at will, he did so anyway. Grants of land from the royal demesne and the hereditary possession of royal offices were extorted from both claimants. Thus a great baron, Geoffrey de Mandeville, was created earl of Essex by both Stephen and Matilda, received extensive grants from the demesne, had a number of lesser barons placed in his vassalage rather than the king's, and became hereditary sheriff of Essex, Hertfordshire, London, and Middlesex and hereditary royal justice in those four counties. He also was made hereditary constable of the Tower of London, was allowed to build a number of castles, and was given permission to tear down a castle that annoyed him

belonging to the bishop of London. Geoffrey was one
of the most successful baronial grabbers, but others
followed the same policy. The great barons built up
independent local positions strong enough so that they
could defy the royal government. They made treaties
among themselves like independent princes.

Henry of Anjou

In 1149 Count Geoffrey of Anjou relinquished the
duchy of Normandy to his son, Henry, who was duly
proclaimed duke. Two years later Geoffrey's death
made Henry count of Anjou. In 1152 he acquired the
vast duchy of Aquitaine by marrying Eleanor who
had just been divorced by Louis VII. Then in 1153
Henry came to an agreement with King Stephen. Stephen was to rule England as long as he lived, his son
William was to receive extensive fiefs in England and
Normandy, and Henry was to succeed Stephen on the
English throne. Thus when Stephen died in 1155,
Henry became king of England. He promptly set to
work to restore the royal government to the position
it had held in his grandfather's time. Henry razed
many of the castles built in Stephen's reign and took
possession of others. He deprived the barons of a large
proportion of the lands and privileges that they had
extorted from Stephen and Matilda. Once more men
of lower rank, mere servants of the crown, replaced
the great barons as sheriffs and constables of royal castles. Once more the king's justices rode through the

land, and the exchequer collected and accounted for the revenues of the crown. Within a few years of his accession Henry had regained what was lost during Stephen's reign and was ready to move forward toward further development of the royal power.

King Henry II found several means by which he could increase his resources as feudal suzerain of England. He advanced the doctrine that he had feudal privileges not enjoyed by other lords. When a knightly family held fiefs from two barons, each baron had the right of custody over the lands held of him at the death of the vassal, and the baron from whom the family had held a fief the longest had the right of marriage. But Henry claimed that when a vassal held a fief directly from him, no matter how small the fief or how recently acquired, the crown had the right of marriage and custody of all the lands. Then when the vassal of a baron died, the baron was obliged to accept the homage of the heir at once and then collect the relief as best he could. But Henry maintained that he had the right to refuse to give a baron's heir possession of the fief until the relief had been paid. The king also attempted to make the military service due him more valuable and to increase the yield of such feudal aids as the aid to knight his eldest son. Most English barons had enfeoffed more knights than they owed the crown under the quotas established by William I. Thus when the king levied an aid at a certain sum for each knight's fee, they made a profit. When the king summoned his

host, they brought the knights they owed and collected a sum of money called scutage from the others.
Henry was determined to share in the profits accruing
from the increase in the productivity of the land and
from inaccurate assessments of service. He held a
great inquest to discover how many knights had been
enfeoffed by his barons. He then tried to levy aids on
all their fees. Although he was eventually forced to
accept a compromise, he greatly increased the service
owed the crown.

The Increase of Royal Power

Henry II did not content himself with developing
his resources as feudal suzerain—he devoted even more
attention to building up his power and revenue as king.
His most important step in this direction was to increase the jurisdiction of the royal justices who trav-
eled over England to hear pleas of the crown. According to English customary law there was only one
method by which a criminal case could be brought
into court—an appeal or accusation by the injured
party or someone acting in his behalf. Under this system many crimes were bound to go unpunished.
Whoever brought an appeal into court was subject to
severe penalties if he lost the case. Hence no one was
inclined to mention the murder of friendless men of
little importance. In all probability there were many
cases that never were brought to court because of fear
of the accused and his friends. The solution that Henry

devised for this problem is still in use today—the jury of presentment.

In a decree known as the Assize of Clarendon, Henry directed that twelve men from each hundred and four from each township should appear before his justices to declare what crimes had been committed in their districts since his coronation and to name those whom they suspected of having committed them. Those accused were to be arrested and obliged to prove their innocence by the ordeal of water. This consisted of being bound and thrown into water. The man who sank was innocent; the one who floated was guilty. These proceedings were carried on with an elaborate religious ritual that made the ordeal a judgment of God. But Henry seems not to have had complete confidence in the result of such a test. He provided that if the man who cleared himself by the ordeal was generally believed to be guilty, he should leave England forever. One obvious result of this new procedure was to increase the number of criminal cases brought to court and improve the maintenance of law and order, and it also increased the king's revenue. When a culprit was hanged, the king seized all his movable property and could "waste" his land for a year and a day. If the man accused by the jury of presentment escaped arrest, he was outlawed and his property seized. Moreover, if the jurors failed to mention a crime that the justices knew about from some other source, they were severely fined.

The invention of the grand jury was an important step in the development of English law. The direct ancestor of the modern petty jury or trial jury grew out of this system. When a man who was accused of a crime by the jury of presentment knew he was innocent and felt certain that his neighbors knew it too, he would "place himself upon the country." The sheriff would then gather a jury of the man's neighbors. If they stated that they believed him innocent, he was freed. In this way the man who felt sure that he was innocent could escape the ordeal.

The Royal Courts

King Henry made use of similar devices to extend the civil jurisdiction of the royal courts. Under English law there was but one way to determine the ownership of property—trial by battle. If both contestants were vassals of the same lord, the battle was fought before his feudal court. If they held of different lords, it was conducted before the shire court. Henry decreed that the defendant in such a case could go to the royal chancery and purchase an order moving the trial to the king's court. Then the sheriff levied a jury of twenty-four knights, called a "grand assize," who were to investigate the question and be ready to state in court which party was in the right. Obviously the holder of property who felt sure that his title was sound would prefer this procedure to the very hazardous and uncertain trial by battle.

In addition to the grand assize Henry invented pro-

cedures known as "possessory assizes." The peace and
quiet of the English countryside was continually being
disturbed by powerful men who believing they had
claim to land ejected by force the weaker men who
were in actual possession of it. King Henry resolved to
suppress this type of disorder. When a man was ejected
from land in his possession without a proper judicial
decision, he could go to the royal chancery and buy
what was called a "writ of novel disseizin." It directed
the sheriff to collect twelve men who would appear
before the king's justices to state whether the plaintiff
had been ejected by force without a court order. If
this assize said that he had been, the sheriff would put
him in possession again. If the man who had seized the
land illegally believed that it was really his, he could
bring a regular suit over the ownership to be tried by
battle or by the grand assize. A similar writ called
"mort d'ancestor" could be used by an heir to obtain
any property that had been in his father's possession at
his death.

The possessory assizes increased the business of
the royal courts by the innovation of new processes.
No existing court was harmed by this. In general the
same can be said of the jury of presentment—it
brought into court cases that would otherwise
never have been brought to trial. The grand assize,
however, took business from both the feudal and the
shire courts that had handled the conventional procedure of trial by battle. And although no official
decree authorizing such a policy has been preserved,

it is clear that Henry encouraged his justices to inter-
fere in other ways with the work of the feudal courts.
If a widow who felt that her husband's heir had not
given her an adequate dower failed to get satisfaction
in her lord's court, she could obtain a writ from the
chancery summoning the case before the king's justices. If a lord refused to accept the homage of a man
who claimed to hold land from him, he could be summoned to explain his action to the royal justices. The
feudal courts continued to function, but they did so
under the realization that their decisions could be
questioned in the king's court.

The legal innovations of Henry II marked the real
beginning of the English common law. The king's
justices enforced the same law throughout the realm.
Before Henry's reign this common law had dealt only
with a few types of cases such as appeals of crimes
reserved to the crown. The feudal courts and popular
courts that did most of the judicial business of the
realm each had its own customary law. But as Henry
extended the jurisdiction of the royal courts, he increased the scope of the common law. Late in his reign
or early in the reign of his successor, one of his justices wrote a treatise on the law enforced by the royal
courts—the book known to us as Glanvil's *De legibus*.

The Constitutions of Clarendon

Another primary concern of Henry II was to define
and stabilize the relations between church and state.

In 1164 he issued for this purpose the Constitutions of Clarendon. In this decree the boundary between the jurisdiction of the royal and ecclesiastical courts was carefully defined. Clerks accused of crimes were to answer before the king's justices. The decision as to who had the right to present a rector to a church or whether or not land was held in free alms belonged to the royal court. Actions for the recovery of debts even when payment had been guaranteed by a religious oath were to be held in lay courts. The church's power of excommunication was limited. No tenant in chief of the crown or royal official was to be excommunicated without due notice to the king or his justiciar. Inhabitants of the royal demesne were not to suffer this penalty until the king's local agent had received notice. Other clauses affirmed the king's rights as feudal suzerain over church lands and their holders. Prelates who held by barony were to perform all the obligations of barons except that they did not have to sit in the king's court when sentence of death was passed on a culprit. It was assumed that they did not owe personal military service. When a bishopric, abbey, or priory fell vacant, the crown was to have custody of its lands. The new prelate was to be elected by the "more powerful persons of his church" in the king's chapel with the king's consent. He was to perform homage and swear fidelity to the king before his consecration.

The archbishop of Canterbury, Thomas Becket, at

first accepted the Constitutions but later denounced them. This led to a bitter quarrel between the king and the primate. For some years Thomas lived in exile in France. Eventually peace was made between the two contestants and Thomas returned to Canterbury, but in reality it was impossible to reconcile the two points of view. Thomas believed that the church should be free from lay control while Henry insisted on the predominant rights of the royal government. One day a messenger came to Henry's camp in Normandy to inform him of some arrogant act of the archbishop, and the king made some impatient remark about his rival. Three of Henry's knights immediately left for England and murdered the archbishop in his own cathedral. King Henry drove the murderers into exile and did abject penance for his part in the offense. On the whole it seems unlikely that he ordered the murder. It is more probable that the knights were personal enemies of the archbishop who seized what appeared to be a good excuse for his assassination. Thomas was a proud, arrogant, ambitious man who had made many enemies. But his death was most convenient for the king—for the rest of his reign the church dared not oppose him. Although the English king did not succeed in obtaining jurisdiction over clerks accused of crimes, most of the questions dealt with in the Constitutions of Clarendon were decided in his favor. The Constitutions were never formally accepted by the church, but in general they governed English practice.

Henry's sons, Richard I and John, continued his policy of developing the royal power. Richard met with no serious opposition. As he led a crusade to Jerusalem and suffered severely for the cause of the Holy Land, the papacy and the church as a whole were inclined to favor him. His personal charm and his reputation as the ablest soldier of his day kept his barons quiet if not contented. But John was far less fortunate. He was fully as determined as his father to maintain and increase the royal power at the expense of its two chief rivals, the church and the baronage. He was able, industrious, and imaginative. Unfortunately he lacked the reputation for personal valor that was so important for a monarch of his day, and he never learned how to make men respect him as well as fear him. In addition, he faced two external foes of unusual quality—Philip Augustus, king of France, and Pope Innocent III; and before he had been king for five years, he had lost Normandy, Maine, and Anjou.

Pope Innocent III

John then entered into a long and bitter controversy with Innocent III over the succession to the archepiscopal seat of Canterbury. This quarrel was extremely complicated in detail, but the main issue was extremely simple. John maintained that no election to an English see was valid without the king's approval. The pope insisted that an election held in Rome in his presence required no such approval. Even-

tually John gave way. He accepted Stephen Langton
as archbishop of Canterbury. Moreover, he surrendered his realm to the pope to be held in the future as a
fief from the papacy. Thus he not only settled his quarrel but gained a firm friend. Innocent III was completely devoted to expanding the power and prestige
of his great office. To acquire the king of England as
a vassal was a decided achievement. Actually John
was merely clearing his flanks for action on another
front. Ever since his loss of Normandy, Maine, and
Anjou, he had been planning to recapture them. He
had built up a large war chest. Part of this had come
from pressing to the fullest extent the financial rights
of the crown. He had demanded enormous reliefs
from his barons and sold privileges to them at a high
price. He had collected scutage without actually carrying out the campaign for which it was intended. He
had used relatively new forms of taxation—income
and property levies and customs duties. Then a fair
part of this war chest represented money extorted
from the clergy during John's quarrel with the pope.
When Innocent placed England under interdict and
forbade the performance of religious services, John
had seized all the church property and had enjoyed
its income for several years. Although when he made
peace with the pope he promised to repay all this
money, he succeeded in keeping a fair part of it. With
these funds John had bought the alliance of a number
of German princes, headed by his nephew the Em-

peror Otto, and of several vassals of the king of France. But his plans came to nothing. King Philip's victory at Bouvines ended John's hopes of recovering his fiefs on the continent.

Baronial Opposition to the Royal Power

The steady development of the royal power under Henry II, Richard, and John was deeply resented by the barons. John's loss of Normandy lowered his prestige and encouraged thoughts of revolt. The situation was further aggravated by John's vigorous and successful attempts to raise money. High reliefs, the demand of large sums for privileges, heiresses sold at exorbitant prices, frequent scutages, and too heavy income and property levies all extracted money from the baronage. During his quarrel with the church John kept most of his barons loyal by sharing the plunder to some extent and by convincing them that a papal victory would harm them as much as him. But his eventual surrender to Innocent III lowered his prestige still further. There were several abortive baronial plots and the great lords showed a decided disinclination to participate in the great attack on Philip Augustus. John gambled everything on the success of this campaign. Had he won, he would have been the master of western Europe and could either have crushed or have bought off his barons. When he returned defeated from Poitou in the autumn of 1214, a baronial rising was almost a certainty.

There is no doubt that in 1214 the vast majority of the barons of England disliked and distrusted King John and were deeply disturbed by his political and financial practices. But an actual revolt needs leaders. These were supplied by a small group of lords, perhaps thirty, whose grievances were particularly serious. Some of these men may have had personal reasons for their hostility to the king; our material is too scanty to allow us to know this for certain. Most, however, had actually been charged enormous reliefs or had paid vast sums for some castle, manor, or right they believed to be theirs by inheritance. Thus each baronial leader hated the king for a specific reason and wanted to gain some definite end such as the possession of a strong castle or an hereditary office. There lay at first their weakness. It was hard to get the baronage as a whole excited about the grievances of the leaders. The solution was supplied by the new archbishop of Canterbury, Stephen Langton. Langton was one of the great canon lawyers of his day. He believed that both clerical and lay society should be governed by orderly, recognized systems of law. He persuaded the leaders of the rebellious barons to draw up a list of general demands that would benefit the feudal class as a whole. The result was the Articles of the Barons —the basis of Magna Carta. John was caught unprepared by the rising. He needed time to gather troops from Poitou and Gascony, put his castles in a state for defense, and appeal for aid to his overlord the pope.

As a result, on June 15, 1215, he accepted the baronial demands, and royal clerks were put to work drawing up the solemn document that would give them the force of law—Magna Carta.

Magna Carta

Magna Carta falls into four chief divisions. The first was primarily feudal and dealt with the king's rights as suzerain. The relief due from a barony was set at a fixed sum. Rules were laid down for the custody of fiefs in the king's care during the minority of an heir, for the treatment to be accorded to a baron's widow, and for the marriage of heiresses. Only one provision of this part of Magna Carta was to have a lasting effect—the king promised not to levy taxes not regularly provided for by feudal custom without the counsel of an assembly of all his tenants in chief. It seems unlikely that such an assembly ever met—it would have been a hopelessly unwieldy body—but the king did in the future always ask the advice of some council before levying such a tax. The next part of the charter was concerned with various practices of the royal administration: how the crown should and should not collect the debts due it, how the constable of a royal castle should get supplies, and how frequently the king's judges should journey about the country to hear the possessory assizes. A third part was of purely temporary interest—it provided the machinery by which the baronial leaders hoped to get the lands and castles they wanted. The fourth part of the Great Charter is, however, still of considerable interest. It laid down certain basic principles that we still value. The chief of these was contained in the thirty-ninth article—"No free man shall be taken, or imprisoned, or deprived of his land, or outlawed, or exiled or in any other way destroyed nor shall we go against him or send against him except by legal judgment of his peers or by the law of the land." The exact meaning of this passage has been long debated by scholars, but the general purpose is clear—the king cannot take any action against a free man without a judgment by the proper court. It is the origin of the Anglo-American conception of "due process of law."

Almost all the detailed provisions of Magna Carta are of interest only to historians. In fact, most of them were obsolete within a century after its composition. But Magna Carta remained an extremely important document. By issuing it John admitted that he was subject to the established law of the realm. One can argue that the conception of customary law governing the relations between lord and vassals was implicit in the feudal system, but with the exception of the much briefer charter of liberties issued by Henry I, Magna Carta was the first explicit admission of this principle by a feudal monarch. The successors of the barons were fully aware of this. Again and again throughout the rest of the Middle Ages, when an English king showed signs of arbitrariness, he was obliged to reaffirm Magna Carta. Long after its actual provisions ceased to have much meaning, it was used as a symbol of the king's subservience to the law.

Simon de Montfort

During the long reign of John's son Henry III the barons came close to obtaining complete dominance. A revolt led by Simon de Montfort, earl of Leicester, led to the king's capture and the rule of Earl Simon in Henry's name. The barons' program was to impose on the king a baronial council of their choosing and to have this body appoint the great officers of state. Simon recognized that the royal government had become too strong and well established to destroy or even reduce in power. His solution was to have the government controlled by the barons. While Simon was running the royal administration, his fellow barons took advantage of the opportunity to usurp all possible privileges. They forbade the sheriffs to enter their lands, took possession of hundred courts and had them held by their own agents, exercised the right of supervising the frankpledge system in their lands, and in general usurped the privileges of the king's local officials. William de Beauchamp, hereditary sheriff of Worcestershire, combined the shire court with his own feudal *curia*. Richard de Clare, earl of Gloucester, withdrew his vassals from the royal hundred courts and obliged them to attend those under his control.

Thus during Henry's reign both the central and local organs of government fell under baronial control.

The Re-establishment of Royal Power

Under the son of Henry III, Edward I, the English feudal monarchy reached its height. In almost every field of governmental activity Edward made decided progress in solving existing problems and laying strong foundations for later development. He was perhaps the foremost soldier of his day. As a young boy he escaped from the guardians whom Simon de Montfort had assigned to watch him, gathered the royal partisans, and in two overwhelming victories crushed the Montfortian party. He was in North Africa on a crusade when his father died, but so complete was the baronial respect for the weight of his sword that England waited in peace and quiet while he made a leisurely journey home.

Edward resolved to put an end to the perpetual border wars with the Welsh. For centuries the Welsh had been raiding the English border and English kings had been conducting punitive expeditions against them. The heavily armed English knights could parade through the valleys of Wales at will, but the Welsh simply took to the hills where the knights could not follow. Edward decided to conquer Wales and keep it subdued. He gathered his feudal levy: his knights and mounted sergeants. With these he drove the Welsh into their hills. Then he levied great numbers of infantry in the shires nearest Wales. They drove the Welsh into the inner fastnesses of their mountains. Around this high mountain section of North Wales Edward built a line of castles and garrisoned them with hired troops, some Gascon mercenaries but mostly English shire infantry. Several times the Welsh broke out, and the contest was long and bitter, but by the end of his reign he was master of Wales and had organized it into shires.

Edward was almost as successful in Scotland. The direct line of the Scots kings ran out and Edward was called upon to arbitrate among the many claimants to the throne. His jurists decided in favor of an English baron, John de Balliol. Edward obliged John to do him homage and to accept him as overlord of Scotland. When John yielded to pressure from the Scots and disobeyed the English king, Edward invaded Scotland. At the end of his reign his troops were in complete control of the lowlands. Edward died as he was crossing the border to crush a Scots rebellion led by Robert Bruce, who was eventually to free Scotland and become its king.

It was Edward I who first developed the longbowmen that were to be the most effective soldiers in western Europe for several centuries. He and his captains also worked out the tactics required for using knights and bowmen together that were to give England so many victories in the Hundred Years' War. Edward found the English army a feudal host occasionally reinforced by mercenary bowmen. He built up a body of English infantry drawn from the men of the shires.

The Royal Prerogatives

Edward also turned his attention to recovering the royal rights that had been usurped by various barons during his father's reign and to preventing further usurpation. He sent out writs of *quo warranto* (by what right) ordering every lord who claimed any special privilege to appear before the royal justices, list the rights he claimed, and prove that he possessed them legally. This could be done either by presenting a royal charter granting the privilege or proving that his ancestors had enjoyed it in the reign of Richard I. Actually Edward had no, intention of pressing the matter quite so strongly. Vague statements that a right had been enjoyed as far back as anyone could remember were usually accepted. Only in the case of recent and flagrant usurpations did Edward deprive a baron of his privileges. But he had effectively put an end to usurpation. In the future a lord could not hope to claim a privilege that had not been allowed him in these inquests unless he had a recent grant to show.

One of the most serious problems that faced the royal government was the growing complexity of the feudal system. Every time a lord gave an estate to a younger son or a marriage portion to a daughter he created a new fief. There could be six or seven lords between the actual holder of a manor and the king.

This made the enforcement of feudal obligations extremely difficult. Edward determined to put an end to this process of creating new rear fiefs, but he did it by a rather indirect method. There was no legal way by which land could be sold. If a man wanted to buy a piece of land, the only method by which it could be done was to pay the holder to grant it to him as a fief. As a man's right to diminish his son's inheritance by granting fiefs was limited, such an arrangement could well be invalid. What was usually done was to arrange a suit in court. The man who wanted to buy the land sued the holder for it. The holder came to court, admitted the plaintiff's claim in return for a sum of money, and the deal was legally registered before the justices. To end all this Edward provided that land could be sold, but when this was done it became a separate fief held of the higher lord. Thus if a baron sold a manor or gave one to a daughter as a marriage portion, it became a fief held directly of the king, not of the grantor. This put an end to the process of subinfeudation that had been going on since the Conquest.

The Statute of Mortmain

Closely related to the problem of the complexity of the feudal system was that of the growing possessions of corporations, especially religious ones. It had long been the custom, when a grant was made in free alms, for the lord and overlords—including the king himself—to renounce the secular service due from the lands so given. Thus if a rear vassal gave a knight's fee to an abbey, the baron and the king lost their feudal service due from it. Worse yet, by no means all such grants were made in good faith. Sometimes a man gave land to a church and thus was relieved of the service due for it. He then received it back for a nominal rent. This practice had been forbidden in an early reissue of Magna Carta, but it was hard to check. Edward decided to secure complete control of all acquisitions of land by corporations. The statute of *mortmain* provided that no land could be given, sold, or rented to a corporation. If it were, it became forfeited to the lord of the giver. Now actually no one seems to have expected that any such absolute prohibition would be enforced. The king could grant dispensation from a statute. Hence in practice this law simply meant that a corporation could acquire land only with the king's permission.

The Exchequer and the Curia Regis

Legislation such as we have been discussing was an important feature of Edward's reign and has led some writers to call him "the English Justinian." The progress made in the development of the organs of government was equally significant. The central administration of the Norman kings, William I, William II, and Henry I, had been carried on by their household officers. The chancellor was the king's chief spiritual adviser and wrote his letters. The chamberlain looked after the royal chamber and also guarded the money and documents kept in a chest at the foot of the bed. Henry I had felt the need for a treasury fixed in one place rather than following the court. He had detached three chamberlains to guard his treasure in Winchester castle. Soon one of these was known as the treasurer and the other two as chamberlains of the exchequer. Henry's treasurer set up a regular system for auditing the accounts of the king's officers and others who owed him money. Twice a year the treasurer and the two chamberlains were joined by other household officers to hold this official audit. At one of these sessions the official annual account, the pipe roll, was drawn up. Between exchequer sessions the treasurer and chamberlains guarded the king's money and paid it out at his order. The men who met with them to audit the accounts were called the barons of the exchequer. Then under Henry I, and particularly Henry II, royal justices became a part of the central administration. In fact, the same men performed both functions, sitting as barons of the exchequer one day and as royal justices the next. But by the time of Edward I these organs had become specialized. There were a treasurer, two chamberlains, and a group of barons of the exchequer who handled the king's financial business. Then there were two royal courts. The court of common pleas sat at Westminster and heard civil cases between subjects—cases in which the

crown had no interest. The court of king's bench consisted of a group of justices who followed the king. It
heard serious criminal cases and any others of interest
to the crown.

In all feudal states it was assumed that the suzerain
would seek the advice of his vassals on important matters. In questions of major importance the English
kings had summoned their full feudal *curia*, the prelates
and barons of their realm. But in lesser matters they
had simply sought the advice of their household
officers and any barons who happened to be at court.
Historians have used the terms "great" and "small"
curia regis to distinguish these two bodies. But once the
judges and exchequer officials had become specialized
it was difficult for the king to seek their advice—
especially when he was not at Westminster. Edward
established a group of specialized advisers, men who
took a special oath to give good counsel. This sworn
body of counselors was the ancestor of the privy council.

The Chancellor and the Privy Seal

One royal office, that of chancellor, grew rapidly in
importance and was in fact divided between several
officials. The chancellor was responsible for the royal
seal that guaranteed the authenticity of the king's
letters. Under the early kings he followed the court
and saw to the sealing of royal letters. But when the
exchequer was established, it needed a royal seal almost

continuously to issue summonses to the king's debtors. Hence, a duplicate seal was kept at the exchequer in the care of a deputy of the chancellor. This official later became independent as the chancellor of the exchequer. Then as time went on the chancellor acquired too many duties to allow him to follow the court. The chancery was established at Westminster and the great seal was kept there. The king had a privy seal and an officer called the keeper of the privy seal. When the king wanted to issue a solemn document, his clerks drew it up, the keeper affixed the privy seal, and it was sent to the chancery where it was made out in final form under the great seal.

Meanwhile the chancellor had acquired important new duties—he had become a high judicial officer. According to the theory of the day the king was subject to the law, but as he was also the source of all law enforcement it was difficult to make his subjection a reality. When the king did something unjust either directly or through an official, the only recourse was to appeal to his conscience. The chancellor was the king's conscience. Those who felt they had a grievance against the king or his officers appealed to the chancellor. Moreover, cases continually arose in which injustice seemed to have been done but for which there was no applicable law. Such cases could be carried to the chancellor and he could see that justice was done. He thus became the earliest judge of what we call equity.

The Development of Parliament

Perhaps the most significant feature of Edward's reign was the development of Parliament. We have seen that the early kings on important questions sought the advice of their feudal court. Acts such as the Assize of Clarendon were issued with the advice of the prelates and barons of the realm. When John wanted to levy a new kind of tax, an income and property tax, he sought the approval of a similar body. Magna Carta provided that no scutages or special aids could be levied without the counsel of a body composed of the prelates and the king's tenants in chief. Although it seems doubtful that all tenants in chief ever met, Henry III regularly sought the approval of his prelates and barons before levying taxes that were to be paid by them and their tenants. Then Simon de Montfort introduced a new element. He was in general more enthusiastically supported by the lower members of the feudal class than by the great barons; therefore on one occasion when he needed popular support he directed every shire court to elect knights who would represent it at the meeting of the council of prelates and barons. But there was one important part of England that had no connection with prelates, barons, or elected knights of the shire—the royal demesne. Although this royal demesne included some rural manors, its most important elements were the royal towns headed by the city of London. The demesne had always been taxed separately from the rest of England. There the king as seigneur had levied tallage. In actual practice he had bargained with the towns to get the largest sum he could. Usually it was a matter of separate arrangements with each town, but there had been times when the king bargained with representatives of all the towns.

In 1295 King Edward I brought all the various elements of his realm together in what historians call the Model Parliament. Individual writs of summons were sent to the archbishops, bishops, abbots, earls, and barons. Each bishop was instructed to bring with him the dean of his cathedral chapter, his archdeacons, an elected representative of the chapter, and two representatives of the clergy of his diocese. Thus the clergy as a whole were represented. Then each shire was ordered to elect two knights and each borough two representatives to sit in the Parliament. In short, the Model Parliament was the direct ancestor of the present English Parliament. The representatives of the lower clergy soon ceased to come, but they are still summoned. The churchmen preferred to hold their own meeting known as a convocation and vote the king money there. As the bishops and abbots were barons as well as prelates they continued to be summoned and to attend with the lay lords. From Edward's point of view the Model Parliament was an ideal body. It represented all the realm—clergy, lay lords, and the royal demesne. Hence taxes granted by it could be collected throughout England.

The fact that the Model Parliament had been held did not mean that all parliaments summoned by Edward had the same composition. The word "parliament" meant essentially a meeting—a talking. A gathering of the prelates and barons could be called a parliament. So could on occasion a meeting of the knights chosen by the shires. Even when all the groups were summoned, most of the business could be done by the great lords before the knights of the shire and the representatives of the towns arrived. Nevertheless the general pattern was set and the conception of a "full parliament" well established.

The primary purpose of the king in calling a parliament was to gain the support of his people—usually their consent to taxation. But once a parliament had met, it could make demands on the king. When a king needed money, he was likely to make concessions to persuade his parliament to grant him the taxes he needed. But Parliament had other functions than merely voting the king money. It soon took the place of the old *great curia regis* as the body to be consulted on all important occasions. Perhaps the most important of these was when the king wanted to add to the law of the land.

The Common Law and Legislation

The common law of England had its origin in the law enforced by Henry I's justices in the few types of cases that came within their jurisdiction, and this law was greatly enlarged by the legislation of Henry II, such as the Assize of Clarendon. This legislation was enacted with the consent of the feudal court of prelates and barons. But Henry's judges and their successors under Richard and John found ways to make new law without formal legislation. The new types of actions invented in Henry's reign were brought into court through writs issued by the chancery. Thus if a man had been forcibly ejected from his land, he obtained a writ of novel disseizin that brought the case before the king's justices. If a widow felt that she was being deprived of her just dower, she sought a writ of dower that brought her plea into the royal court. Hence, when the justices saw a situation that seemed to them to require a legal remedy, they were inclined to invent a new writ. By this method the common law and the jurisdiction of the royal courts expanded very rapidly. But in the reign of Henry III the barons called a halt to this process. They insisted that additions to the common law must be made by formal legislation. Such formal legislation was known as a statute. Although it is clear that in the reign of Edward I statutes were being made by the prelates and barons alone when they met as a parliament, before long it was generally understood that statutes could only be made in full parliament.

CHAPTER III

The Empire 〰〰〰〰〰〰〰〰〰

THE basic social and political structure of the East Frankish kingdom ruled by the descendants of Louis the German was far different from that of the West Frankish state that fell to the successors of Louis' brother, Charles the Bald. Except for Lorraine, which Louis had acquired at the death of his nephew, Lothaire II, none of the lands that composed his kingdom had been part of the Roman Empire for any considerable time. Only Lorraine and Franconia had formed a permanent part of the Merovingian state. The major part of the kingdom, Bavaria, Swabia, Thuringia, and Saxony, had been added to the Frankish state by the early Carolingians.

In the western kingdom the counts administered districts the boundaries of which were those of the Roman *civitates*. In the eastern kingdom the count was the king's personal representative with vague power of supervision over a group of local popular courts, but there were no stable, organized counties. Vassalage, which had become an important part of the institu-

tions of the western kingdom, hardly existed in the
eastern outside Lorraine and Franconia. Thus the East
Frankish state was in general a region of free landholders, large and small, noble and peasant, who ruled
themselves through the popular courts under the
supervision of the counts. In Bavaria, Swabia, and Saxony there was a certain amount of local patriotism
among the people, going back to the days of their independence before their conquest by the Franks. The
royal power rested on the king's control over the
counts, on the royal estates scattered over the land,
and on the king's right to choose the bishops and abbots
who held the vast church estates.

The Tribal Duchies

Although the eastern kingdom suffered little from
Viking raids, it faced fully as formidable a foe—the
savage Magyar horsemen from the Hungarian plain.
Before the death of Louis the German they were
plundering Bavaria, and by the end of the ninth
century they had extended their operations over most
of Germany. Louis' descendants found themselves
completely unable to defend their kingdom effectively. Hence, there appeared in Bavaria, Swabia, Franconia, and Saxony local military leaders who used the
remnants of tribal patriotism to organize resistance to
the Magyars and to establish themselves as regional rulers. These leaders took the title of duke, and their
duchies are often called "stem" or tribal duchies. The

ambition of each duke was to absorb the royal authority in his duchy—to control the counts, choose the
prelates, and usurp the royal estates. During the reign
of the last Carolingian king, Louis the Child, who
ruled from 899 to 911, the dukes came very close to
achieving their purpose.

The extinction of the line founded by Louis the
German might have meant the end of the East Frankish kingdom had it not been for the church. The prelates of Germany not only believed in monarchy as an
institution, but they were also convinced that the
safety of their estates depended on a strong king.
During the reign of Louis the Child the dukes had freely usurped ecclesiastical estates in order to build up
their own landed power, and lesser nobles had followed their example. The church felt very strongly the
need for a crowned and anointed king who would be
its ally and curb the greed of the nobles. In general, like
the great lords of France, the dukes had no desire for a
strong king and would have been pleased to have no
king at all, but in the year 911 they too were inclined
to seek a national leader. The Magyar raids were at
their worst and all Germany except Saxony had suffered from them. Without a king organized resistance
was almost impossible, as no duke could be persuaded
to act unless his own duchy was being invaded. Hence,
the dukes joined with the prelates to elect a king—
Conrad, duke of Franconia.

Unfortunately Conrad was not a strong king. As a

military leader he failed to check the Magyars, who carried their raids as far as Bremen in northern Germany. He also lacked the resources needed to curb the dukes. As the Carolingian estates had been largely usurped during the reign of Louis the Child, Conrad was obliged to rely on his own duchy, and Franconia was far weaker in material and human resources than the other stem duchies. The dukes of Saxony, Swabia, and Bavaria ignored the king and went on consolidating their power. By the end of Conrad's reign each duke wielded full royal authority within his own duchy, and the king was a mere figurehead. Conrad saw the situation very clearly. He realized that if a strong German monarchy was to be developed, it must be done by the most powerful of the dukes. Therefore as he lay on his deathbed he designated Henry, duke of Saxony, as his successor and directed his younger brother to secure Henry's succession to the throne.

The House of Saxony

Saxony was by far the strongest of the stem duchies. Entirely untouched by the feudal institutions that were beginning to spread from Franconia into southern Germany, it was a country of noble and nonnoble free landholders. These men made excellent soldiers and were completely devoted to their ducal house. Thus the Saxon kings had a firm and adequate nucleus for their power. The five monarchs of this dynasty were to rule Germany for over a century, 919–1024. They were to develop and consolidate the royal power in Germany itself, direct the first attempt of the Germans to expand over the lands between the Elbe and the Oder, and revive in a new form the conception of the empire.

The first task of the Saxon kings was the expulsion of the Magyars. Although Henry I defeated them in battle and limited the extent of their raids, this menace to Germany was ended only by his son Otto I's great victory of the Lechfeld in 955. This battle freed the Bavarian Ostmark, modern Austria, from the Magyars, and some years later it was erected into a separate frontier province ruled by a royal appointee. With the reconquest of this region the Germans reached their permanent frontier on the southeast.

The Royal Power

The chief concern of all the Saxon kings was the development of their power in Germany. Saxony itself was never given to a younger son but was held firmly in the hands of the crown. When the younger brother of King Conrad died in 939, his duchy was taken over by Otto I. With Saxony and Franconia supplying them with a solid base, the kings were able gradually to reduce the authority of the dukes of Swabia and Bavaria. The royal estates usurped by the dukes were recovered and the counts were brought directly under the king's control. Moreover, feudal

ideas were introduced into the relationship between
the king and the dukes—the latter were obliged to hold
their offices as royal vassals.

Placing the counts directly under the control of the
crown served to weaken the dukes but did not supply
the king with reliable local agents, since the counts
were nobles who were chiefly interested in increasing
their own lands and power. To supply this deficiency
the Saxon kings turned to the church. As we have seen,
the prelates of Germany had been the chief supporters
of the monarchy in its period of weakness in the late
ninth century. The church maintained vigorously the
conception of the king as a ruler appointed by God—
rex et sacerdos. Hence, a close alliance between crown
and church was perfectly natural. The first step of the
Saxon kings was to recover the power of appointing
bishops and abbots that had been usurped by the dukes.
Then the kings took the prelates and their lands under
their protection. The estates of the church were removed from the jurisdiction of the counts, and special
royal agents called advocates exercised the comtal
authority there under the supervision of the prelates.
Finally in many cases the king gave a prelate one or
more counties. The ancient duchy of Franconia was
practically divided between the bishops of Wurzburg
and Bamberg. This system greatly strengthened the
monarchy. A bishopric could not become hereditary,
and the king could in general make certain that it was
held by a man who could be trusted. The prelates be-

came the chief local agents of the crown, and a large part of the royal army was drawn from the church estates. In short, this alliance between crown and church was the primary base of the power of the Saxon kings outside their own duchies of Saxony and Franconia.

Conquest in the East

As their duchy of Saxony was the chief source of their power, Henry I and Otto I were deeply interested in extending its frontiers. Henry carried out a series of campaigns by which he forced the Slavic tribes on the eastern border of his duchy to accept him as overlord and pay him tribute. Otto went much farther. He conquered the region between the Elbe and the Oder and filled it with well-garrisoned fortresses. Although these burgs were thickest in the March of Thuringia lying to the east of that province, they were also scattered over the whole countryside. Otto kept a tight hold over the southern part of the conquered region, and its margrave, Gero, was simply his agent, but in the nothern section he gave a free hand to a great Saxon noble, Hermann Billung.

Just as Otto and the church were allies in consolidating the royal power, so they worked together in subduing the Slavic tribes. When Otto conquered a tribe, he obliged its members to pay tithes to the church. He founded new bishoprics in the conquered territory and endowed them with vast grants of land. In 962 he established the archbishopric of Magdeburg.

According to the arrangement made with the pope, this see was to have no eastern boundary so that it could cover any Slavic lands Otto or his successors might conquer.

Unfortunately, the German conquerors, laymen and ecclesiastics alike, were both greedy and cruel. They collected all the profits they could, and any resistance was punished by savage massacres. As a result, in 983 when Otto II was occupied in Italy, the Slavs rose in a general revolt and drove out their German masters. Except for the thick mass of fortresses in the western part of the March of Thuringia, all the new burgs and episcopal seats were destroyed. The German colonization of the region between the Elbe and Oder was thus postponed until the twelfth century.

The Middle Kingdom

Under the Saxon kings Germany was by far the most powerful state of western Europe, and it was only natural that its rulers should desire to control the fragments of Lothaire's middle kingdom—Italy and the borderlands between Germany and the western kingdom. This was not pure imperialistic ambition. The royal power of the German kings was largely centered in the north in Saxony and Franconia. If a rival house, especially if it were the ducal house of Swabia or Bavaria, could combine Italy and the kingdom of Burgundy, it could build up a position in the south that would seriously threaten the power of the

Saxon kings. This menace almost became a reality in 926 when Rudolf, king of Italy and Burgundy, attempted to succeed his father-in-law as duke of Swabia. When Rudolf died, his lands fell into confusion, with fierce civil war between rival claimants. The dukes of Swabia and Bavaria both extended their lands to the southward and waited hopefully for an opportunity to seize all or part of Rudolf's inheritance. Otto could not permit this to happen. He seized Burgundy in the name of Rudolf's son Conrad, who later ruled that kingdom as his vassal. Then in 951 he invaded Italy, assumed for himself the Lombard crown, and married Rudolf's daughter. Eleven years later he was solemnly crowned emperor by the pope and thus founded what is usually called the Holy Roman Empire.

There is no reason to suppose that Otto I thought that he was reviving the empire of Charlemagne, much less the Roman Empire in the West. Neither he nor his successors made any attempt to extend their power over the West Frankish state. Otto believed that the safety of the German kingdom demanded that its rulers control the middle kingdom once possessed by Lothaire. As Lothaire had been emperor, that dignity constituted to some extent a title to those lands. This was particularly important while vassals of royal rank ruled the Burgundian kingdom. In short, Otto became emperor in the interest of his German kingdom and never showed much concern for Italy. His only at-

tempt to develop his power in that kingdom consisted
of an extension of his policy of close alliance with the
church. He made important grants of lands and privileges to the bishops of northern Italy in the hope of
winning their loyalty to his dynasty. Except for his
grandson Otto III, or rather the ministers who ruled
in his name, the later Saxon emperors showed the
same lack of interest in Italian affairs. They sought to
maintain their authority in Italy by winning the support of one of the factions struggling for power in
that kingdom. Sometimes they would favor the bishops and at others the great lords. This policy was never
strikingly successful. When the emperor was in Italy
with a German army, he was the master of the land. In
his absence the local factions struggled for supremacy.
The ministers of Otto III followed a different policy.
They attempted to develop a strong government by
importing German officials, but the effort was not
sufficiently prolonged to be successful. Essentially the
Saxon emperors were German kings who simply
wanted to be sure that no one else dominated Italy.

The Salian Dynasty

In 1002 the death of Otto III brought to an end
the senior line of the Saxon dynasty. Although his successor, Henry II, is usually considered a member of
the Saxon line because he was the head of a junior
branch of the house, Henry was a south German lord
whose power lay largely in Bavaria. The death of

Henry in 1024 was followed by the election of Conrad, called the Salian, the descendant of a daughter of Otto I, as king. Conrad's power was centered in Franconia and Swabia. He was the founder of the Salian line that was to rule Germany and the empire for just over a century.

Within their German realm the Salian kings faced different problems from those that had given concern to their predecessors. The Saxon monarchs had largely devoted their energies to breaking the power of the stem duchies and assuming direct royal authority over the counts and prelates. In this they had been entirely successful. The dukes had failed to turn their military leadership into territorial power, and Germany had become a united state instead of a loose confederation of autonomous duchies. But the Saxon kings had worried little about the rapidly growing power of the aristocracy. The counts and great landholders were directly dependent on the king, yet he could not effectively control them. In short, the Saxon kings had nothing that can be called an administrative system. Their power rested essentially on their personal prestige, the strength of the monarchical tradition, and their success in placing their friends among the aristocracy in important positions. But the nobles as a whole enjoyed almost complete independence as long as they did not actually rebel against the crown. Their power was based on lands that they owned. Although many nobles, especially in Bavaria and Franconia, held both the office of count and fiefs granted to them as vassals, these were incidental additions to their basic resources. By the time of Conrad II some of these nobles had become extremely powerful and were fully as dangerous to the monarchy as the old stem dukes had been. Thus, in Saxony members of the house of Billung were practically the masters of the lands between the Weser and the Elbe and were serious rivals to the royal authority in Saxony. The Welf family had built up a somewhat similar position in Bavaria and Swabia. But these two families were simply the most noted examples of successful aristocratic enterprise. All over Germany nobles great and small were developing local centers of power and almost complete independence of effective control.

Administration of the Realm

The Salian kings saw that if the monarchy was to maintain its position against the nobles, it needed firmer bases for its power. The primary requirement was effective royal agents who were devoted to the crown. For this purpose Conrad II began to use a peculiarly German institution—*ministeriales*. These were nonfreemen who were employed for knightly functions. The idea apparently originated in the German church. When the Saxon kings insisted that the church supply knights for their army, it did so by giving lands to unfree tenants in return for knight service. Thus land was given in return for service as in western feudalism, but the fact that the holders of the fiefs were unfree prevented them from claiming the ordinary rights of vassals. The land remained in full possession of the church, and its holder could be displaced at any time. Conrad put royal *ministeriales* in charge of the estates of the crown. His successors were to use them to garrison castles, hold important offices, and in any other capacity that seemed necessary. By this means the Salian kings hoped to establish a royal administration independent of the aristocracy and devoted to the service of the crown. This device was not essentially unlike the later Capetian practice of using men drawn from its towns as officials, but the *ministeriales* were even more dependent on their master than the townsmen.

In addition to a loyal bureaucracy the monarchy needed a strong territorial base that was strategically located from a military point of view. The original center of the power of the Salian house lay in Franconia. By extending its direct control over Thuringia and southern Saxony it could hold the strategic heart of Germany. This plan had several incidental advantages. A center of royal authority in south Saxony would serve to curb the most dangerous of the rising noble families, the Billungs. But of still greater importance was the fact that the Harz mountains contained valuable silver mines. By ruling that region the crown could secure a money income that would add greatly to its strength.

The Development of Saxony

Henry III chose Goslar as the seat of royal authority in south Saxony and built a strong castle there. His
son Henry IV decided to make Goslar the permanent
capital of his kingdom. There he built a palace that is
probably the best extant example of eleventh-century
civil architecture and then set to work to turn the
whole country around Goslar into a great royal military stronghold. South Saxony and Thuringia were
filled with royal castles garrisoned by devoted *ministeriales* drawn from distant estates of the Salian house.
In addition, Henry carried on a vigorous campaign to
restore the rights enjoyed by the Saxon kings in their
duchy. He revived long forgotten payments and services due from the Saxon freemen and enforced the
royal monopoly of the forests.

The policy of the Salian kings was deeply resented
by all elements of Saxon society. The Billungs objected
vigorously to having a center of royal power within
what they considered their sphere of influence. The
nobles as a whole despised the lowly born *ministeriales*
and considered it outrageous to have them command-
ing royal castles, administering crown lands, and even
acting as ministers of state. The free peasants were
aggrieved by the revival and rigorous enforcement of
ancient ducal rights. The result was a series of Saxon
rebellions between 1070 and 1075. Henry IV's *ministeriales* held his castles vigorously, and the rest of Ger-

many supported him. The Saxons were defeated and their rebellion crushed. Thus in 1075 Henry IV seemed well on the way to building a strong German monarchy and creating a unified German state. At a time when William the Conqueror was just beginning the formation of the English monarchy and the Capetian kings were helpless feudal overlords, the king of Germany had a fixed capital, a secure money income, and an efficient and loyal body of crown servants.

The Church and the State

Unfortunately, just as Henry was ready to complete and solidify the work of the Salian house, a storm that had been brewing for some time burst suddenly about his head. In a letter of December 8, 1075, Pope Gregory VII threatened to depose Henry unless he made full submission to the papacy. This was not only the first step in a long and bitter struggle that was eventually to destroy the German monarchy but it was also the first definite announcement of an entirely new conception of the relationship between church and state.

As we have seen, during the ninth and tenth centuries the church had consistently preached the sacred character of kingship. The king was appointed by God to rule and his anointment by the church gave him a priestly character—he was *rex et sacerdos*, king and priest. The church had as a matter of course supported the kings with all its resources. It seems likely that it was this alliance between crown and church that had saved the French monarchy from extinction, and it was the chief bulwark of the power of the Saxon kings of Germany. It had also safeguarded the material possessions of the church from the greedy warriors of western Europe and had brought to the prelates extensive political privileges and powers. In short, throughout Europe and particularly in Germany the alliance had been to the material advantage of both parties. But it had not in general been beneficial to the spiritual development of the church. Prelates were chosen largely because they could be useful to the king as statesmen, warriors, and local agents. Few kings showed any great interest in the spiritual qualifications of their appointees. Moreover, these prelates were as a rule interested in the development of their own and the royal authority and cared little for the position of the church as a whole. Thus the alliance between crown and church had led to the almost complete secularization of the church. Except for his costume it was hard to tell a bishop from a baron.

The Cluniac Reform Movement

The foundation of the abbey of Cluny in 910 inaugurated an attempt to check the secularization of the regular clergy. With Cluny as its center a great wave of monastic reform spread over western Europe. As the monasteries were not of too great political importance, this phase of the Cluniac movement was well received by most lay lords and the order grew with astounding rapidity. Then early in the eleventh century ecclesiastics who were imbued with the Cluniac spirit of reform began to turn their eyes toward the secular church. Here too, in Germany at least, they soon found an enthusiastic lay ally. The Emperor Henry III was convinced that church reform was his chief duty. Moreover, his position enabled him to start the reform where it was most needed—with the papacy itself.

The Saxon emperors had treated the papacy as they had treated other Italian factions: sometimes as an ally, sometimes as a foe. Occasionally they had intervened to place their own candidates on the papal throne and always had insisted on their right to confirm papal elections. Their interest in the papacy was purely political, as one of the powers that had to be managed in order to maintain the imperial authority in Italy. But Henry III believed that the papacy alone could lead a general reform of the church, and he placed a series of reforming popes on the papal throne. These men began the construction of the great papal monarchy that was to play so important a part in the history of the next three centuries. Their object was to reform the church by making it subject to strict papal control.

Henry III seems to have failed to realize that this movement was bound to threaten the alliance between crown and church in Germany. His intention was to

have reforming popes and reforming bishops all chosen
by him and loyal to him as well as to the cause of reform. Many of the reforming clergy agreed with this
point of view. They saw the divinely appointed king
working hand in hand with the papacy to raise the
spiritual level of both the clerical and lay worlds. But
others felt that effective church reform depended on
complete independence from lay control. The pope
must be the sole master of the church. As it was most
unlikely that the lay rulers would agree to this, this
branch of the reform party was in reality committed
to a campaign against the secular rulers.

The Investiture Controversy

During the latter years of the reign of Henry III and
the minority of Henry IV the leader of the radical
reform party was an Alsatian ecclesiastic named Hildebrand. His purpose was to remove the church from
lay control, place it firmly under the authority of the
papacy, and make the pope the acknowledged head
of Christendom. To him the king was not divinely appointed and had no sacred character. He was a sort of
police chief to be elected by his subjects to rule as
long as he ruled properly. If he ruled improperly, he
could be removed by Christ's vicar, the pope. Hildebrand probably inspired the establishment of the college of cardinals as an electoral body in order to end
imperial control of papal elections. In 1073, some
eight years after Henry IV attained his majority,

Hildebrand became pope as Gregory VII. He promptly issued a decree insisting that bishops be elected in accord with the canons of the church and denying the king's right to invest them with the symbols of their office. If carried out, this would immediately break the king's control over the German church. Although Henry IV was planning a new basis for the power of his monarchy, he had no intention of giving up the system that had served his ancestors so well, and he ignored the pope's order. The result was the letter of 1075 threatening him with deposition.

It would be futile to attempt a detailed account of the long and bitter contest between Henry IV and Gregory VII. It was a war fought for political ends with both spiritual and secular weapons. Pope Gregory had as allies the Norman kingdom of Sicily, the powerful countess of Tuscany, and the majority of the lay aristocracy of Germany. Henry had the support of the loyal servants of the Salian house and the majority of the bishops of Germany and Lombardy, who had little enthusiasm for reform and less desire to be controlled by the pope. Henry's reply to Gregory's letter threatening him with deposition was to gather his clergy at Worms and declare that Gregory should be deposed as a false pope. Gregory thereupon excommunicated Henry and absolved his subjects from their allegiance to him. The German nobles then rose and informed Henry that unless he received absolution they would proceed to elect a new king. Henry crossed the Alps, rallied his Lombard allies, and found the pope at the countess of Tuscany's castle of Canossa. There after a humiliating show of penitence he was absolved.

The nobles of Germany, however, proceeded to elect a new king, who was soon killed in battle. A fierce civil war waged in both Germany and Italy ended with Pope Gregory's flight from Rome and his death at Salerno in the Norman kingdom. But Gregory's successors continued to foster revolt in Germany, and the rest of Henry's reign was occupied by civil strife—much of it against his own rebellious sons. Henry died in 1106 and was succeeded by his son Henry V, who was able to restore peace in Germany and make some progress in carrying on his father's domestic policy. The investiture controversy, the nominal cause of the struggle between empire and papacy, was settled in 1122. German bishops were to be elected by the cathedral chapters in the presence of the emperor or his representative, who was also to invest the newly elected prelate with the insignia of his temporal office. In short, the German king could continue to control episcopal elections.

The Age of Castles and Communes

The civil wars that accompanied the investiture controversy had profound effects on the social and political structure of both Germany and Lombardy.

In Germany the anarchy resulting from civil strife led to rapid development of feudal and manorial institutions. Every nobleman with sufficient resources built a castle from which he could dominate the countryside and plunder his weaker neighbors. The only safety for minor nobles lay in becoming the vassals of more powerful ones. The ordinary freeman had two choices: he could become the vassal of a noble or sink into serfdom on some noble's manor. The *ministeriales* shook themselves free from their servile bonds and became vassals. Yet the feudalization of Germany was not complete as it was in England and France. The greater lords retained the lands they had held in full ownership, but many of them held fiefs as well. The lesser nobles were largely forced to become vassals holding their lands as fiefs. All, high and low, built castles and, under one excuse or another, usurped full rights of jurisdiction over the inhabitants of their lands. The nonnoble freeman who had been such an important element in German society practically disappeared. Even the prelates took part in this scramble for feudal power. They raised troops by enfeoffing knights and forced the minor nobles in their neighborhood to become their vassals.

In Lombardy it was Henry's allies, the bishops, who suffered from the civil strife. Their vassals rebelled against them and formed sworn associations or communes to exercise the political authority once held by the bishops. These communes were scattered over the countryside in both rural and urban communities, but as the cities were the seats of the bishops, the urban communes were far more powerful than the rural ones. Once they had broken the power of the bishops, they began to extend their authority. The rural nobles who had not at first joined the communes were forced to do so or were deprived of their lands. Only a few very powerful lords were able to remain independent of the dominance of the city communes. Thus Lombardy became a land of city-states governed by local aristocracies.

Although Henry V made some attempt to continue the policy of his father in Germany, he was in general helpless before the growing power of the nobles. When he died childless in 1106, the great lords pointedly ignored his designated heir, his nephew Frederick of Hohenstaufen, duke of Swabia, and elected as king Lothar of Supplinburg, duke of Saxony. This step was clearly intended to weaken the monarchy by making it elective. Actually, Lothar was unable to exercise any effective power. He owed the throne to the great lords and held it only by continually granting them lands and privileges. Moreover, his rival Frederick of Swabia refused for years to recognize him as king and carried on a fierce civil war against him. The story of these two rival houses illuminates the history of Germany in the late eleventh and early twelfth centuries. The father of Frederick of Hohenstaufen was a minor Swabian noble who was successful in developing his power during the civil wars of Henry IV's reign and eventually married the king's daughter, with whom he received the title of duke of Swabia. Lothar of Supplinburg was another successful upstart who at the death of the last Billung duke of Saxony had obtained that duchy on the ground that his mother was a Billung. In short, the nobles of Germany were choosing their kings from their own ranks without regard for hereditary right. This process was repeated at Lothar's death in 1137. Lothar had designated as his heir the head of the great house of Welf, his son-in-law Henry, duke of Bavaria, but the great lords elected instead Conrad, brother of Frederick, duke of Swabia. Again they were successful in obtaining a weak and pliable monarch who gave them no serious trouble.

The Houses of Welf and Hohenstaufen

During Conrad's reign there was almost continuous strife between the houses of Welf and Hohenstaufen. The death of Lothar had made Duke Henry of Bavaria duke of Saxony with the result that his resources exceeded those of the crown. When he died in 1139, he was succeeded by his very able son Henry, called the Lion, who was one of the great figures of German history. The weak and colorless Conrad could do little more than try to stir up rival nobles to annoy Duke Henry. When Conrad died in 1152, even the German aristocracy was tired of civil strife and sought a king who could restore order. Their choice fell on

Conrad's nephew, Frederick of Hohenstaufen, duke of Swabia. From the point of view of the nobles Frederick was the ideal candidate. By passing over Conrad's son they were able to affirm the elective principle. Yet the man they chose was both the effective head of the house of Hohenstaufen and a first cousin of Henry the Lion. Actually the nobles had chosen better than they intended; they had elected one of the great men of the age.

Frederick I of Hohenstaufen, usually called Barbarossa from his red beard, faced extremely difficult problems. The whole structure on which the Saxon and Salian state had rested had disappeared, and he had to construct a new monarchy on new bases. Even the political theories that supported the royal and imperial authority had to be revised to meet the high pretensions of the successors of Gregory VII on the papal throne. Here Frederick showed no hesitation in taking the offensive. The revival of the study of Roman law made available the political ideas on which the Late Roman Empire had been based. Frederick was not content to be merely king and priest—he was the sacred emperor and God's regent in Christendom. To emphasize this continuity between imperial Rome and imperial Germany he arranged for the canonization of Charlemagne. But Frederick had no intention of carrying this line of thought too far. The Roman emperors had been elected at least in theory by the Roman Senate. Charlemagne had been crowned by the pope and the papal party argued that he had been given the imperial title by the pope. The famous forgery, the Donation of Constantine, by which the pope was granted the rule of the western half of the empire, was a powerful weapon in the papal arsenal. Frederick brushed all this aside. He was entitled to all the powers of the Roman emperors, but his right rested on conquest. The German kings had won the empire by the sword.

An Imperial Policy

Frederick I was the first German king whose policy was essentially imperial and who devoted the major part of his attention to his non-German lands. In Germany he was content to force the great lords to recognize their feudal obligations to the crown and to leave them to rule their vassals. As long as he was not faced with actual rebellion, he left the German princes to pursue their own courses. He himself turned to the thorough subjugation of Italy. Historians have explained this policy in two strikingly different ways. Some have concluded that Frederick was overcome by his own political theory and was filled with imperialistic dreams. According to these writers, he sacrificed his opportunity to build up an effective government in Germany to his desire to be master of Italy. The other view is that Frederick had little choice and followed the only practical course. The royal demesne of the Salian kings had disappeared during the civil wars. Outside his duchy of Swabia, Frederick was simply the feudal suzerain of the German princes, and any attempt to build up direct royal power based on demesne and castles seemed utterly hopeless. Even in Swabia Frederick's power was not too solid. Although he held the ducal title and had extensive demesne, much of the duchy was in the hands of powerful vassals who were almost as independent as the other German lords. The revival of trade and commerce had, moreover, made Lombardy an extremely rich and prosperous region. If he could get it firmly in hand and draw a large revenue from it, he would have a sound base to operate from. Combining Swabia, Burgundy, and Lombardy would give him an integrated territorial power. In short, according to this school of historians, Frederick's only chance of effectively controlling Germany was to develop overwhelming power in the imperial lands outside the German realm.

The Lombard League

Soon after his accession Frederick set to work to reestablish the imperial power in Lombardy. His object was to see that the officials who ruled the communes were either his appointees or elected officials confirmed by him with the understanding that they ruled as his agents. He also demanded fixed money payments to swell the imperial treasury. For a time he was successful. Although Milan gave some trouble, most of the towns accepted Frederick's terms. The emperor then turned his eyes southward, and his agents began to demand imperial dues in Tuscany and the Romagna. This brought on an immediate clash with the papacy. The pope had been troubled by the development of imperial power in Lombardy, but he was thoroughly alarmed when Frederick invaded the Patrimony of St. Peter. The conflict became sharper when in 1159 a new and more strongly anti-imperial pope ascended the papal throne. The new pontiff immediately renewed the traditional alliance between the papacy and the Norman kingdom of Sicily and began to incite the Lombard towns to revolt. Milan grasped the opportunity, rose in rebellion, and was utterly destroyed by the enraged emperor. Frederick filled Lombardy with fierce German knights who ruled with a heavy and barbaric hand. The result was a general alliance of all the Lombard towns: the Lombard League. Frederick retired to Germany and mustered a great army with which to crush the Lombard cities, but in 1176 he was utterly defeated by the forces of the League in the battle of Legnano. His only course was to make peace. By an agreement reached in 1183 the communes received full rights of self-government. They did, however, admit that they were vassals of the empire and agreed to pay an annual rent for the imperial functions exercised by their officials. Lombardy remained a source of revenue, but it was not a base for imperial political authority.

In the treaty of 1183 the Lombard League agreed

to aid Frederick in recovering his imperial rights in the rest of Italy. Two years later he made a formal alliance with Milan for this purpose. Hence, although he had been checked in Lombardy, he continued to develop an effective imperial administration in Tuscany, the Romagna, Spoleto, and Ancona. Except for a few great cities such as Florence, Siena, and Pisa that were placed on an equal footing with the Lombard communes the towns of these regions were placed under German officials. By the end of Frederick's reign central Italy was ruled by German imperial officers and paid taxes to the imperial treasury. To strengthen his position in this region he came to an agreement with the Normans and his son Henry married a Sicilian princess. His arrangements in central Italy had but one serious weakness: they had been made in defiance of the papacy and were not recognized by it. This troubled Frederick very little, but it was to be a serious problem for his successors. Otherwise Frederick had been completely successful in establishing in central Italy the firm basis for his imperial power that he had failed to find in Lombardy.

Henry the Lion

During the early years of his reign Frederick kept on good terms with his cousin Henry the Lion. He even gave him the fortress of Goslar and its territory as a fief, thus rounding out Henry's duchy of Saxony. But as the years went on Duke Henry grew more and more powerful. A series of successful campaigns against the Slavs had added to his lands much of the territory between the Elbe and the Oder formerly conquered and lost by his Billung ancestors. His marriage to an English princess, a daughter of King Henry II, increased his prestige. Moreover, he had taken advantage of Frederick's quarrels with the papacy to usurp the lands of Saxon prelates who supported the pope. Frederick decided that Henry was becoming too powerful and in 1168 deprived him of Goslar. From that time on the two cousins were bitter foes. Henry was waiting until a good opportunity appeared for successful revolt, but that opportunity never came, for by 1180 Frederick was ready to strike. Duke Henry was ordered to restore the church lands he had seized. When he failed to obey, he was summoned to the king's court. His failure to answer this summons resulted in his condemnation and the loss of all his lands. Frederick divided Saxony in half. The western part, known as Westphalia, was given to the archbishop of Cologne, while the eastern section was granted Bernard of Anhalt, a great-grandson of the last Billung duke. Bavaria was given to Otto of Wittelsbach, whose descendants ruled it until 1918.

The crushing of Henry the Lion was not inconsistent with Frederick's general policy of strengthening the greater lords of Germany. He simply did not want one man to be too powerful. In fact, his action in giving Henry's lands to others instead of turning them into royal estates seemed to give sanction to a principle that had long been favored by the great nobles—that lands once granted by the crown as a fief could not be taken into the demesne again. It was indeed Frederick who really started the German princely class by giving his tenants in chief special privileges that raised them above the rank and file of the nobility. Thus he organized a definite and recognized feudal hierarchy and turned the German monarchy into a feudal state. Within Germany the king became a feudal suzerain with few resources under his direct control. This was not too serious as long as the monarchs had extensive resources outside Germany to bolster their power, but it meant that the loss of those outside resources would doom the crown to impotence.

The Kingdom of Sicily

Frederick Barbarossa died on a crusade in 1190 and was succeeded by his eldest son, Henry VI. As the husband of Constance of Sicily, Henry was already deeply involved in Italian politics. At the time of her marriage it was agreed that Constance should be queen of Sicily if her nephew, King William II, should die without children. But the idea of being ruled by a German prince was repugnant to the Sicilian barons, and when William died in 1189 they chose as king Tancred, count of Lecce, an illegitimate son of Constance's younger brother Roger. As soon as he mounted the German throne, Henry proceeded to assert his claims on Sicily. Tancred managed to hold his own until his death in 1194, but his son William was unable to hold at bay Henry's German army and soon the latter was master of the Norman kingdom.

Obviously from one point of view the acquisition of Sicily was a tremendous gain for the house of Hohenstaufen. It was a highly organized and efficient feudal state with a large revenue. At the same time its possession involved certain serious disadvantages. The Sicilian kingdom was part of the Mediterranean world, and the interests of its kings had been centered in that area. Even their ambitions to make conquests in Greece were inherited by their German successor. Although Henry never actually took any action in this direction, his plans for it diverted his attention from problems nearer home. Moreover, it was almost impossible to hope that the papacy could be reconciled to having one monarch rule all Italy. Sooner or later such an arrangement was bound to reduce the pope to the status of the chief prelate of the empire. Finally the solidification of his position in Italy was certain to require most of Henry's attention and resources at a time when the domestic problems of Germany were calling for consideration. With the acquisition of Sicily, Henry became essentially an Italian king, whether or not he himself was conscious of the fact.

Henry realized that his chief need was to come to

an agreement with the papacy. He offered the pope
a large annual revenue in return for the abandonment
of the papal claims to the Romagna, Ancona, and Spoleto. But he refused to consider giving up the Sicilian
crown and even declined to do homage to the pope
as had the Norman kings. Naturally the pope would
not accept the offer. It meant giving up a large part
of the papal states and reconciling himself to the idea
of a unified Italian kingdom. Not even Henry's plea
that he planned to lead a great crusade could move the
pontiff.

Next to obtaining papal recognition of his position,
Henry's chief desire was to persuade the princes of
Germany to make the kingship hereditary, thus safe-
guarding the succession of his young son Frederick.
This the princes absolutely refused to do, but they
finally agreed to elect Frederick king while his father
lived and so in theory at least insure his succession.
Thus the princes kept the elective principle intact
while granting Henry his immediate desire. Unfortunately for the house of Hohenstaufen, the infant king
was to succeed all too quickly. Less than a year after his
son's coronation Henry VI died in Sicily.

At first it appeared that the premature death of
Henry VI would not seriously affect the Hohenstaufen regime. The German imperial officers in Italy
and Sicily seemed able to hold their own, and Henry's
brother Philip, duke of Swabia, declared himself regent for his young nephew. Philip was an able man

who was respected throughout the empire, and he was enthusiastically accepted by the majority of the German princes. Soon, however, he found himself facing the ancient foes of his house—the Welfs and the papacy.

The Pontificate of Innocent III

Early in 1198 Innocent III ascended the papal throne. He was a man of strong and dominant character who had great ability and was thoroughly imbued with the most exalted ideas of the papal office. He believed, probably correctly, that the independence of the papacy required the possession of a strong secular state and a divided Italy. He therefore set to work to regain the lost parts of the Patrimony of St. Peter and to separate the empire from Sicily. While he recognized young Frederick of Hohenstaufen as rightful king of Sicily, he encouraged the Sicilian barons to eject Henry's German officials and to rule the kingdom themselves in the name of their infant lord. But as he was determined to prevent the uniting of the empire and Sicily, he could not accept Philip of Swabia as regent of the empire.

Actually it seems unlikely that the pope alone could have given Philip much trouble. But unfortunately the Welf, or rather the anti-Hohenstaufen, party in Germany was still in existence, headed by the powerful archbishop of Cologne. The second son of Henry the Lion, Otto, was living in England and was high in

favor with his uncle, Richard I. Richard's bitter foe
was King Philip Augustus of France, and for some
years he had been subsidizing the German princes of
the Rhine valley in order to gain their aid against the
French king. Naturally it occurred to Richard that
it would be very convenient to have his nephew master of Germany. Hence Otto set out to seek the German throne well supplied with pounds sterling. On
July 12, 1198, he was crowned king by his partisans.
This convinced the princes who supported the house
of Hohenstaufen that the empire could not survive a
long minority, and they persuaded Philip of Swabia
to accept the crown. Thus Germany had three coro-
nations in two years—young Frederick of Hohenstaufen in 1196 and Otto and Philip in 1198.

Even with the aid of funds from England Otto
found it impossible to make any headway against
Philip of Swabia, and in 1208 he retired to England.
Innocent III was so thoroughly discouraged with his
failure that he prepared to come to terms with Philip.
But suddenly a fresh stroke of misfortune came upon
the house of Hohenstaufen—King Philip was assas-
sinated by a private enemy. The German princes immediately re-elected Otto, and he marched to Rome
where Innocent placed on his head the imperial crown.
The pope soon found that he had miscalculated. As
an adventurer seeking the German throne, Otto had
cheerfully promised the pope the return of the lands
he claimed. As emperor, he immediately took up the

policy of Barbarossa and Henry VI: not only did he make clear to the pope that he meant to keep the imperial lands in central Italy, but he proceeded to invade the kingdom of Sicily. Innocent found himself faced with a difficult choice. He could allow Otto to become master of the empire and Sicily, hoping for some later chance to retrieve the papal position, or he could depose him and support an antiking. But the only rival with any chance of success was Frederick of Hohenstaufen, and his triumph would also combine the empire and Sicily. Innocent waited eight months before coming to a final decision. Then he excommunicated Otto and threw all his power behind the cause of Frederick. We can only guess at the pope's reasons. Otto was a mature man who would be hard to change. Frederick was still a boy who was at least nominally a papal ward. He might perhaps be molded. Then, despite his arrogance and ambition, Innocent was a firm believer in justice. Frederick was undoubtedly the rightful king of Sicily, and as a minor he was in the wardship of his suzerain, the pope. Innocent could hardly stand by and allow Otto to conquer his ward's kingdom.

Frederick II of Hohenstaufen

Frederick's success was rapid. The Hohenstaufen party in Germany rallied around him, and King Philip Augustus—who knew that Otto and his uncle King John of England were planning a joint invasion of

France—made an alliance with Frederick and loaned him a large sum of money. In December, 1212, Frederick was crowned at Mainz. On July 27, 1214, the crushing defeat of Otto by King Philip at Bouvines left Frederick master of Germany. The son of Henry VI was the ruler of the vast lands of his father.

Frederick II had spent his boyhood in Sicily, and his interest centered in that realm. He liked the sunny skies and considered Germany a hopelessly cold, wet, and gloomy land. He was a man of great personal attainments—a poet and a patron of poets, a scholar and a patron of scholars. He was almost completely free from the bonds that held other men of his day. He was entirely irreligious and purely secular in his interests and points of view. He had few morals, either public or private. Frederick not only kept a harem but he had Moslem ladies in it. When he went on a crusade, he promptly made friends with the Moslem foes of Christendom and obtained a highly advantageous peace without any fighting. All this deeply shocked and fascinated his contemporaries. In short, Frederick was an extremely versatile man with a colorful personality, who had a delightfully romantic and on the whole unfortunate career.

Although Frederick had promised Innocent III that he would give the crown of Sicily to one of his sons and keep its government separate from that of the empire and had renewed this promise several times thereafter, he could not bring himself to give up the land he loved. Yet he did make a genuine effort to

come to terms with the papacy. He returned to papal
control the lands of central Italy that the pope claimed.
But having made this concession he felt obliged to
find other resources elsewhere in Italy and decided
to attempt to bring Lombardy fully under imperial
authority. This alarmed the pope almost as much as
had his possession of central Italy. Even the enlarged
papal states would be helpless if caught in a vise between Lombardy and Sicily firmly in the hands of a
strong monarch. Naturally the Lombard towns also
objected to losing the independence they had enjoyed
for so long. Moreover, Frederick wanted no vague
suzerainty. He extended to Lombardy the highly organized royal government that existed in his Sicilian
kingdom. Soon his Sicilian officials were thoroughly
hated throughout the land and the Lombard League
was reformed. Hence, Frederick spent most of his
reign in conflict with the papacy and the Lombard
towns. It is useless to go over the contest in detail. It
is a story of excommunications and absolutions, of
overwhelming victories and crushing defeats. As long
as he lived Frederick had the upper hand, but he never
succeeded in crushing the Lombard League. When he
died, his Italian lands fell into a confusion that was to
last until the nineteenth century.

The Policy of Frederick II in Germany

Frederick's sole interest in Germany was to keep
it quiet so that it would not divert his attention from
his Italian plans. After his final victory over Otto in

1214, he spent less than two years in his northern kingdom. His policy was to give the princes whatever they
wanted to keep them contented. In a series of decrees
he abandoned to them the last vestiges of imperial
authority. The princes both lay and ecclesiastical were
given full power of government in their lands and
guaranteed against any form of royal interference.
The rising towns that had long supported the monarchy were cheerfully abandoned to the mercy of the
princes. Frederick's son Henry, who ruled in Germany for his father, did his best to check this dissolu-
tion of the royal power—he even rose in revolt against
his father. But Henry's position was hopeless as long
as Frederick supported the princes. The natural result
of Frederick's policy was that the princes devoted
their attention to building up their own states and took
no interest in the emperor or the empire. When in the
last years of his reign Frederick desperately needed
German aid in Lombardy, the princes calmly did
nothing.

The death of Frederick II marked the end of royal
government in Germany and imperial government in
the empire. The German monarchy became purely
elective, with the power of the king depending on the
extent and resources of his own princely estates. The
monarchy had no organization, and the king's authority over the princes was almost entirely nominal. Some
of these German kings were to gather armies, march
to Rome, and receive the imperial crown. But at most

their authority in Italy was purely temporary. The great empire of the Hohenstaufens had become a vast maze of independent states.

Before leaving mediaeval Germany it is important to notice that the German kingdom of Frederick II was far larger than that ruled by the Salian kings. The eastward expansion of the Germans that had been halted in the tenth century got under way again in the early twelfth. The Emperor Lothar, his son-in-law Duke Henry of Saxony, and especially the latter's son Henry the Lion had pressed forward the conquest of the lands between the Elbe and the Oder. These princes had done more than subject the Slavs— they had opened the country to German colonization. The civil strife of the investiture contest had led to firm establishment of the manorial system in western Germany and many hardy men were anxious to migrate to new lands. These German colonists were excellent farmers who raised the value of the territory they settled. Hence, Slavic princes were as anxious to obtain them as were the German lords. When the boundary of Germany itself was pushed almost to the Oder, many Germans went on to settle in Bohemia and Poland. Thus while the Hohenstaufen kings were devoting their attention to Italy, the princes and people of Germany were expanding eastward. The mark of Brandenburg, a creation of this movement, was the nucleus of the modern Prussian state.

Conclusion

THIS essay has traced the history of the three great states of western Europe from the tenth through the thirteenth centuries. The three stories have certain common characteristics. Each state started as a Germanic monarchy and eventually became a feudal monarchy. In each state the kings struggled vigorously to develop a strong royal government against the opposition of the baronage. But in each state different circumstances affected this contest and hence the results varied greatly. It is true that superficially the political structures of France and England seemed much alike at the close of the thirteenth century. Each had a strong monarchy that combined the ancient kingly rights with the prerogatives of feudal suzerainty. Each had a highly developed royal government with financial and judicial organs. In each state there existed a representative assembly, an estates of the realm. There were, however, striking differences between the two countries. England was comparatively small in area and population. The members of its feudal class were closely bound together by long years of intermarriage and by their common efforts both in serving and opposing their kings. Although there were great lords and small lords, all held much the same position in

relation to the government and had common interests. English kings had quarreled with their vassals,
but with the possible exception of John no monarch
had ever thought of ruling without their full co-
operation. And by the end of the thirteenth century
most English barons had given up trying to develop
local independence—their aim was rather to control
the royal government. The bureaucracy that served
the English king was extremely small: some dozen
judges and a few financial officers aided by a staff
of clerks. The local royal government was carried on
by sheriffs and other officers who were in general
members of the feudal class. When Edward I nego-
tiated with his people, it was with the "community of
the realm": the peers and representatives of shires and
towns assembled in Parliament. The barons of England might quarrel with the king but not with the
royal government, for of this they were themselves
an integral part.

The French state was molded in a different pattern. It was still an alliance of feudal principalities,
some of which were almost sovereign. The duchy of
Brittany and the appanages of the Capetian princes
were bound to the kingdom only by the fact that their
lords were the king's vassals. In short, the true kingdom of France was the royal demesne. By the close
of the thirteenth century this demesne was large and
its administration well centralized. The French kings
governed through a large and complicated bureaucracy. In addition to the Parlement, the *chambre des*

comptes, and other central organs of government there were the *baillis,* the seneschals, and a host of minor officials scattered over the demesne. These men were the king's servants who lived on his pay. The Estates General was summoned by Philip the Fair to give him the support of his people in his struggle with the papacy, but it was not an integral part of the royal government. The government of France was effective and well organized, but it was something apart from the people.

Nevertheless, despite the divergencies in the political structure of the states, the kings of France and England had succeeded in developing strong monarchies. In this they had been aided by both ability and good fortune. The dynasties that ruled these two states during this period produced a remarkable number of very able men. Moreover, there was little to divert their attention from building up their power. Although the kings of France and England waged fairly continuous war against each other, they had no other dangerous foes. Neither monarchy embarked on large-scale adventures that seriously strained its resources. Neither was ever faced with the necessity of buying the support of its baronage with destructive concessions. Furthermore, they had extremely good fortune in one important respect—serious disputes over the throne were very few. From Hugh Capet to Philip IV the French crown descended from father to son without serious question. In all that long period there were but two minorities and in each of these an able and effective regent ruled with a firm hand. The French monarchy never suffered from the anarchy of a disputed succession and no opportunity was given for a revival of the theory of elective monarchy. The English dynasty was almost equally fortunate. Except for the reign of Stephen there was no period when the English crown was in dispute in any practical form. Duke Robert of Normandy advanced his claims against his younger brothers, William II and Henry I, and Arthur had a reasonable claim against John, but neither of these claimants was taken very seriously in England. There is little doubt that the French and English monarchies owed much of their success to their good fortune in producing male heirs. The serious decline in the power of the English crown during Stephen's reign shows clearly to what end a succession of such disputes might have led.

The German monarchy was far less fortunate than its western neighbors. Only the Hohenstaufens can be charged with deliberately neglecting their interests in Germany in order to develop their power in Italy, but many German monarchs used in Italy time, energy, and resources that might better have been spent at home. Moreover, possession of Italy meant close relations with the papacy. When the popes began their great effort to free the church from secular control, it was but natural that they should first devote their attention to the monarchs nearest at hand. It seems quite doubtful that Gregory VII would have waged so fierce a war against Henry IV merely to free the German church from royal control. What really troubled him was Henry's dominance over the bishops of Lombardy. In short, it seems clear that directly and indirectly the Italian interests of the German kings did much to prevent them from building a strong monarchy at home. But in Germany also the question of succession to the throne played a large part. None of the dynasties that ruled Germany were able to produce sons for more than four generations. Had the line of Henry the Fowler been able to pass the crown from father to son from the tenth to the thirteenth centuries as did the Capetian house, it seems likely that the elective principle would have been forgotten as completely in Germany as in France. And every break in the royal line meant a dispersion of the demesnes and a weakening of the monarchy. Whatever the causes may have been, the result was decisive. The death of Frederick II left the German monarchy destitute of resources and authority. The king of Germany depended for his power on his own resources as a prince, and the electors who chose the monarch were usually careful to see that no very powerful prince received the office. Thus at the close of the thirteenth century Germany was in reality a loose coalition of practically independent states, ranging from important duchies like Bavaria, through small counties such as Wurttemberg and proud free cities like Hamburg and Bremen, to the tiny fiefs of imperial knights. There was no royal demesne, no royal government, and no king except in title.

In closing, a few words seem in order about the standards of royal living and the scale of royal activity in the era of the feudal monarchy. One striking feature was the peripatetic character of the kings and their courts. In the early part of the period the monarch and his entire administration roamed continuously from one demesne manor to another. In England King Henry I fixed his treasury at Winchester, and Henry II established a court to sit at Westminster where the royal treasury had been placed by that time. By the reign of Edward I there were considerable numbers of officials permanently in residence at Westminster, but the king and his court continued to travel about. In France there was no fixed center of the government until after the time of Philip Augustus. That monarch had his treasury in Paris, but it was located in the house of the Knights Templars and served by them. Only under St. Louis can one begin to call Paris the capital of France in any true sense, and the king himself was rarely there. Henry IV built a royal palace at Goslar and apparently planned a permanent capital, but the scheme was forgotten, and the German kings remained ambulatory. The fact that the courts were continually moving prevented them from being very complex. King John of England rarely stayed more than a week in one place. His court was transported by from one to three carts and perhaps a dozen pack horses. He was usually accompanied by several hundred hunting dogs and their attendants. The king had his household seneschal or steward, several chamberlains, several wardrobe servants, a few chancery clerks, a small body of knights and cross-bowmen, and a miscellaneous collection of bath masters, cooks, washerwomen, huntsmen, and grooms. There is some reason for believing that the lines between the washerwomen and prostitutes was not too finely drawn. When the queen accompanied the king, she had her own group of household officials and servants. But the kings were inclined to leave their queens in one place and wander about without them. The royal residences were like those of the great lords. In the early period they would consist essentially of two rooms—a hall and a chamber. Later somewhat more spacious dwellings appeared. But by and large royal life was extremely simple.

It is impossible to give figures for mediaeval incomes that have any meaning today. Royal and noble incomes are peculiarly deceptive because they covered the cost of government as well as private expenses. King John's income from England ranged from £24,000 to £100,000, the variations being the result of special taxes. John's richest vassals may have had incomes as high as £2,500 or even more. But it seems quite likely that a number of great English lords may have had as much to spend on their personal and household expenses as did the king. John believed that his archbishop of Canterbury had more. In short, most of the royal income went into the costs of government. In the time of John, Normandy yielded about the same revenue as England. The demesne of the French kings before the conquest of Normandy seems to have brought in about the same amount. Thus Normandy, England, and the Capetian royal demesne were of about equal value.

Except in regard to residences and mistresses, all the operations of the feudal monarchs were on a small scale. King John had seventy-two castles and a dozen or so hunting lodges. Although one cannot give an exact estimate of his mistresses, he was clearly supplied with them on a scale that would satisfy a western monarch of any age. But his armies were quite small. When he invaded Ireland in 1210, he seems to have led about 1,200 knights and probably half as many crossbowmen. At the battle of Lincoln in 1217, one side had 400 knights and 300 crossbowmen while the other had 600 knights and some 1,000 miscellaneous infantry. By the latter part of the thirteenth century the English kings were using infantry drafted from the shires, and armies grew rather larger. Edward I seems to have had at times as many as 15,000 infantry and 3,000 horsemen.

Compared to the Byzantine emperors, the Moslem caliphs, and their own successors after the Renaissance, the feudal monarchs of Europe lived simply and with few of the trappings of majesty. But one gets the impression that a remarkably high proportion of them were able and vigorous rulers. Certainly the kings of France and England laid firmly the foundations for the future greatness of those states.

Genealogical Tables

Table I. The Carolingians

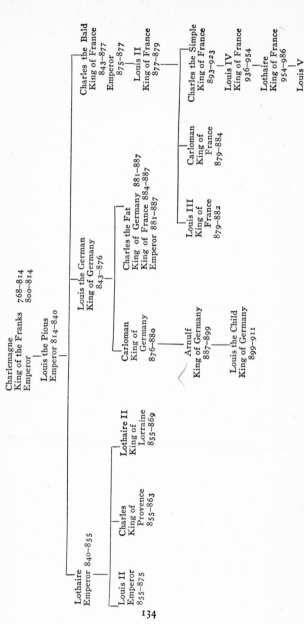

Charlemagne
King of the Franks   768–814
Emperor   800–814

Louis the Pious
Emperor 814–840

Lothaire
Emperor 840–855

Louis II
Emperor
855–875

Charles
King of
Provence
855–863

Lothaire II
King of
Lorraine
855–869

Louis the German
King of Germany
843–876

Carloman
King of
Germany
876–880

Arnulf
King of Germany
887–899

Louis the Child
King of Germany
899–911

Charles the Fat
King of Germany 881–887
King of France 884–887
Emperor 881–887

Louis III
King of
France
879–882

Carloman
King of
France
879–884

Charles the Bald
King of France
843–877
Emperor
875–877

Louis II
King of France
877–879

Charles the Simple
King of France
893–923

Louis IV
King of France
936–954

Lothaire
King of France
954–986

Louis V
King of France
986–987

134

TABLE II. THE KINGS OF FRANCE

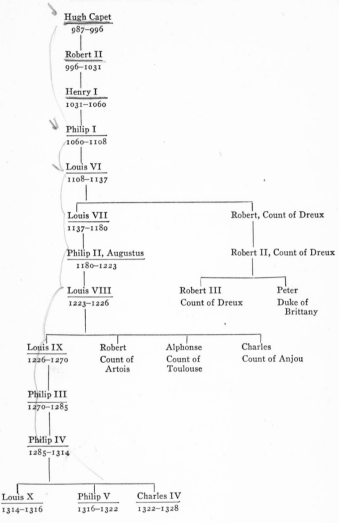

Hugh Capet
987–996

Robert II
996–1031

Henry I
1031–1060

Philip I
1060–1108

Louis VI
1108–1137

Louis VII   Robert, Count of Dreux
1137–1180

Philip II, Augustus   Robert II, Count of Dreux
1180–1223

Louis VIII   Robert III   Peter
1223–1226   Count of Dreux   Duke of
                                       Brittany

Louis IX   Robert   Alphonse   Charles
1226–1270   Count of   Count of   Count of Anjou
             Artois   Toulouse

Philip III
1270–1285

Philip IV
1285–1314

Louis X   Philip V   Charles IV
1314–1316   1316–1322   1322–1328

TABLE III. THE KINGS OF ENGLAND

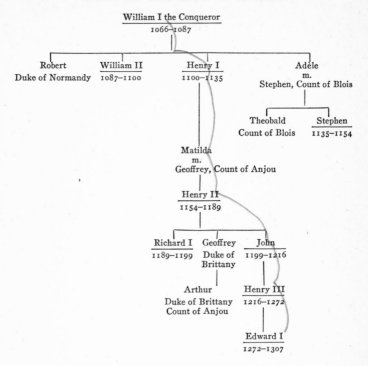

TABLE IV. KINGS OF GERMANY

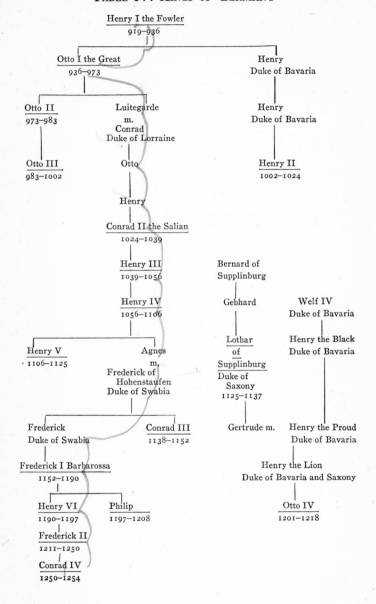

Church & Wars
E Emp
H Ro Emp
Fr Monarchy

Chronological Summary~~~~~

814 Death of Charlemagne.

843 Final division of Carolingian empire.

919 Election of Henry the Fowler as king of Germany.

955 Battle of the Lechfeld.

987 Election of Hugh Capet as king of France.

1066 Norman Conquest of England.

1073 Accession of Pope Gregory VII.

1152 Marriage of Henry, duke of Normandy and count of Anjou, with Eleanor, duchess of Aquitaine.

1164 Constitutions of Clarendon.

1166 Assize of Clarendon.

1176 Battle of Legnano.

1204 Conquest of Normandy, Maine, and Anjou by Philip Augustus.

1214 Battle of Bouvines.

1215 Magna Carta.

1295 Model Parliament.

1302 First Estates General.

1305 Election of Pope Clement V.

Suggestions for Further Reading

THE best general history of mediaeval France available in English is Frantz Funck-Brentano, *The Middle Ages* (New York, 1923). Two recent works in French give excellent up-to-date surveys of the period covered by this essay: Ferdinand Lot, *La France des origines à la guerre de cent ans* (Paris, 1941) and Robert Fawtier, *Les Capétiens et la France* (Paris, 1942). Several works in English are useful for particular phases of this era in French history: A. Luchaire, *Social France in the Time of Philip Augustus* (New York, 1912), C. H. Haskins, *The Normans in European History* (Boston, 1915), and Sidney Painter, *The Scourge of the Clergy, Peter of Dreux, Duke of Brittany* (Baltimore, 1937). The student who can read French would do well to explore either C. E. Petit-Dutaillis, *Etude sur la vie et le règne de Louis VIII* (Paris, 1894) or Elie Berger, *Histoire de Blanche de Castille* (Paris, 1895). Both are excellent works on important periods.

The period in English history with which this essay is chiefly concerned is covered by H. W. C. Davis, *England under the Normans and Angevins,* (10th ed.; London, 1930). The same period is surveyed in greater detail in two volumes: G. B. Adams, *History of England from the Norman Conquest to the Death of John* (London, 1905) and T. F. Tout, *History of England from the Accession of Henry III to the Death of Edward III* (London, 1905). Anyone interested in knowing more about the Anglo-Saxon kings should read F. M. Stenton, *Anglo-Saxon England* (Oxford, 1943). There are two recent studies of the reigns of particular kings: Sidney Painter, *The Reign of King John* (Baltimore, 1949) and F. M. Powicke, *King Henry III and the Lord Edward* (Oxford, 1947). Three biographies of important individuals might be mentioned: F. M. Powicke, *Stephen Langton* (Oxford, 1928), Sidney Painter, *William Marshal* (Baltimore, 1933), and Charles Bémont, *Simon de Montfort* (Oxford, 1930).

The development of the feudal monarchy in both France and England is discussed in an excellent work, C. E. Petit-Dutaillis, *Feudal Monarchy in France and England* (New York, 1936). The student who would like to see at first hand the contemporary attitude toward the French and English kings as well as something of the life of the time would do well to read Joinville's *Chronicle of the Crusade of St. Louis* (Everyman's Library), or Walter Map, *De nugis curialium*, tr. by Montague R. James (Cymmrodorion record series; London, 1923).

Geoffrey Barraclough, *Origins of Modern Germany* (Oxford, 1946) is an excellent recent work covering the entire history of the mediaeval German monarchy. James Westfall Thompson, *Feudal Germany* (Chicago, 1928), contains some theories not now generally accepted, but it is highly readable and is particularly valuable for its description of Germany's expansion to the east. James Bryce, *The Holy Roman Empire* is a classic of historical literature. H. A. L. Fisher, *The Medieval Empire* (London, 1898) is a detailed study of the entire empire and its history. Two valuable biographies are Ernst Kantorowicz, *Frederick II* (New York, 1931) and A. L. Poole, *Henry the Lion* (London, 1912).

Index